Growing into Giving
young people's engagement with charity

Catherine Walker
and
Andrew Fisher

SUPPORTED BY

JOSEPH
ROWNTREE
FOUNDATION

The Joseph Rowntree Foundation has supported this project as part of its programme of research and innovative development projects, which it hopes will be of value to policy makers, practitioners and service users. The facts presented and views expressed in this report, however, are those of the authors and not necessarily those of the Foundation.

Published by Charities Aid Foundation
Kings Hill
West Malling
Kent
ME19 4TA

Tel + 44 (0)1732 520000
Fax + 44 (0)1732 520001
Web address http://www.CAFonline.org

Editor Andrew Steeds

Design and production GreenGate Publishing Services

Printed and bound by Bell & Bain Ltd, Glasgow

A catalogue record for this book is available from the British Library.

ISBN 1-85934-145-4

The CAF research team

Cathy Pharoah (Director of Research)
Catherine Walker (Head of Research)
Liz Goodey (Research Projects Officer)
Andrew Fisher (Research Assistant)
Michelle Graley (Administrator)

Tel + 44 (0) 1732 520125

Web address http://www.CAFonline.org/research

E-mail mgraley@CAFonline.org

Contents

Acknowledgements

This research was carried out by the CAF Research department, and supported by Joseph Rowntree Foundation (JRF). The research team would like to thank JRF for its generous funding of this research and for the input and support of Maggie Jones. The authors would also like to thank Cathy Pharoah, Director of Research at CAF, for her invaluable help and advice during the project.

The project has benefited from the expertise and enthusiasm of an advisory group to whom the authors are particularly indebted. The members of the group included:

Al Cook and Tristan Walker	Oxfam
Laura Edwards	Institute for Public Policy Research
Maggie Jones	Joseph Rowntree Foundation
Priya Lukka	Institute of Volunteering Research
Cathy Pharoah	Charities Aid Foundation
Andrew Spencer	Children & Young People's Unit, Department for Education and Skills (DfES)
Andy Thornton	The Giving Campaign
Jane Tunstill	Royal Holloway College, University of London

Other people and organisations offered invaluable assistance in carrying out this project, and the authors would like to thank:

- Kathy Gaskin, independent consultant, for leading the focus groups in Canning Town and Birmingham, and for allowing the authors to sit in and take notes;

- BMRB International, for carrying out the national omnibus survey of 16–24 year olds;

- CEMS (Centre for Ethnic Minority Studies), for carrying out the focus group with the Islamic Society, Royal Holloway University of London, and for providing their analysis to the authors;

- Stefanie Sonnenberg, for arranging the group in St Andrews;

- CAF Corporate Services, for providing liaison with Loop and Royal & Sun Alliance.

The authors would like to acknowledge all those who helped to set up the focus groups at the following establishments and all those who participated in them:

- Bicton College, Devon

- Iceland Foods, plc., Deeside

- New Deal for Young Unemployed, Community Links, East London

- Royal & Sun Alliance, Liverpool

- Royal Holloway University of London (Islamic Society)

- St Andrews University (Christian Union members and friends), Scotland

- Selly Oak Special School, Birmingham

- Worthing College, Sussex

- Yorkshire Water Services and Loop Customer Services Ltd (subsidiaries of Kelda Group plc), Bradford

- and also a pilot group from Kings Heath Boys School, Birmingham.

Executive summary

Background

Young people's involvement with civil society, and particularly the voluntary sector, appears from all accounts to be worryingly insubstantial. Data from the UK over the last twenty years have shown a decline in young people's participation in volunteering and giving money to good causes. There is much concern that their position may be due to a lack of resonance with, trust in or goodwill towards the voluntary sector, and that this might continue into their adult lives: young people may have a limited capacity to give to charity now, but it is self-evident that the future health of giving depends on the engagement of this group.

Although several studies have looked at young people's disengagement with volunteering and considered other forms of involvement, there has been almost no investigation of the reasons behind the decline in giving money. This research aims to address this specific gap in knowledge, asking young people directly about their current engagement with the voluntary sector in the UK – in particular whether or not they give money – and what they imagine their future engagement will be.

The research was funded by the Joseph Rowntree Foundation and carried out by Catherine Walker and Andrew Fisher of CAF Research (Charities Aid Foundation).

Methodology

The research used both qualitative and quantitative methods. The aim was, first, to allow young people to talk about charity and giving in a neutral setting in a number of focus groups, and to follow this up with benchmarking questions in a nationally representative quantitative survey. Fieldwork for the study was carried out between March and June 2002.

This report details the views of these young people – drawing out the main messages emerging from the discussions and survey data – and uses these messages to make policy recommendations for those involved with young people and the voluntary sector.

Summary of main findings

Perceptions of 'charity'

- Young people's definition of 'charity' and 'giving' goes beyond formal organised charitable activities, focusing more on engagement through active involvement.

- Young people do not see charity as something that only charities do: they also consider informally 'helping' others in the community as an important charitable act. They therefore place a high value on neighbourliness or something akin to citizenship, and consider that giving time in general demands more effort than giving money and is often a more valuable gift.

Giving to charity

- When young people think about spending money, charity is not the first thing they think of spending it on, and many feel that there are more pressing personal calls on their limited financial resources.

- Young people are engaged in a wide variety of activities that come under a broader definition of 'charity'. This engagement, better defined as 'altruistic engagement', ranges from giving goods to charity shops to buying the *Big Issue* and taking part in charity events.

- Young people feel very strongly that they have the same responsibility to give as older age groups do. The survey reveals that they gave an average of £6.94 in one month, which, when relative income is taken into account, compares favourably with national adult giving of around £11.82.[1]

Relating to charities

- Young people feel that charities place too great an emphasis on raising money and that this can be disempowering, since young people have limited finances and have more to offer than money.

- Almost half of the young people surveyed thought there were not enough opportunities to give time, while only one-fifth felt there were not enough opportunities to give money to charity.

- Many young people also feel that they are not presented with opportunities appropriate to their interests and activities.

- Young people are generally positive about charities and their effectiveness in tackling needs by distributing funds, providing care and support, campaigning and raising awareness, and by filling the gaps left by government funding.

---

1 The figure of £6.94 is close to the figure of £6.99 identified in national surveys undertaken by NCVO/NOP. The adult giving figure of £11.82 is from Jas *et al.* (2002).

Future engagement

- Young people want more information from charities about what charities do with their money and how their donations effect change; they believe that more information would encourage them to give more in future.

- The future looks relatively bright: the vast majority of young people say that they will give in future – either money or time, or more likely both. In order for their engagement to be encouraged, however, young people would like it to be easier for them to become more involved. Such engagement is seen as beneficial to both young people and charities.

Implications and recommendations

FOR CHARITIES AND THE VOLUNTARY AND COMMUNITY SECTOR MORE WIDELY

Perceptions of charity

Young people's definition of 'giving' and 'charity' is more inclusive than conventional approaches and includes a broad range of activities (which involve more than just giving money).

Official surveys of giving need to be extended to recognise and measure the real contributions of young people, in all their variety. Charities that address young people only as potential donors are being too short-sighted and risk alienating a group, many of whom already feel marginalized. These charities, and society more widely, need to consider 'charity' more broadly in order to include young people's contributions.

Giving to charity

Young people's engagement in a wide variety of altruistic activities should be celebrated.

There should be greater recognition of such forms of citizenship as recycling, giving goods to charity shops, and campaigning. Charities should recognise what a huge resource young people are, and work out how to use this resource effectively, sensitively, and co-operatively. Charities are the ideal catalysts to engage a generation decreasingly responsive to traditional involvement in society.

Relating to charities

To engage young people, charities need to offer the kinds of opportunity young people will find attractive.

This research has brought to light a specific and conspicuous gap in opportunities for relevant engagement in this 16–24 year group, and identifies this as a possible reason for the apparent lack of engagement of young people. Charities need to find out more about the ways in which young people feel they can make a contribution. They should acknowledge the value of young people's support and look for ways of channelling it that go beyond the giving of money or a narrowly defined set of volunteering opportunities. Charities need to give young people the right kind of opportunities to become engaged in the issues that they are tackling.

Future engagement

Charities need to provide young people with tangible evidence of what they do with their money.

Young people generally believe that charities do good for society, and that giving money, time and other assets to charities are good things to do. They generally trust charities to do the right thing, but they feel that they would be more inclined to give money if they knew what was done with their money – this is particularly true of charities whose work is overseas. Young people should be reassured that their donations have an impact in places where they cannot see this impact for themselves. Getting young people more involved with the whole charitable process could provide opportunities to see this at first hand.

The new citizenship curriculum offers charities further opportunities to engage young people and inform them about their work. Similar opportunities to engage exist in other forms of contact with education, e.g. work experience and sandwich courses. Charities would benefit not only directly from the input of young people in time and effort but also, indirectly, because engagement often leads to greater giving. In addition, by offering more opportunities for young people to get involved on the ground – in the short term or the long term (e.g. volunteering during gap years) – charities may encourage young people to see the voluntary sector as a viable and interesting career path.

THE IMPLICATIONS OF THIS REPORT FOR POLICY MAKERS, TEACHERS, YOUTH WORKERS, AND OTHERS DEALING WITH YOUNG PEOPLE

Young people need to be encouraged to engage with charity on terms that allow them to take the initiative, to be creative and make a difference. The success of the Millennium Volunteers programme has shown that such schemes can promote engagement with the community and foster social capital, thereby reducing social exclusion among young people. Young people have a lot of opinions and ideas about charities and more widely about world events, but feel they do not get the opportunity to express these views very often. The introduction of citizenship into the National Curriculum in September 2002 may help, but teachers, policy makers and youth workers still have an active role to play in putting this and other ideas into effective practice.

THE IMPLICATIONS OF THIS REPORT FOR EMPLOYERS

Young people would be more likely to participate in running charity events organised in or by the workplace if they were given greater opportunity to be involved at all stages, e.g. if they were consulted on the choice of charity and the nature of the event. Using charity events may also be a way for employers to boost employee morale and staff cohesion, as well as enhancing their own reputation.

THE IMPLICATIONS OF THIS REPORT FOR FUNDERS

Evidence from the Millennium Volunteers programme, from research undertaken by the Giving Campaign and from this research has shown that young people are receptive and enthusiastic if approached in the right way. Funders of schemes for young people – such as local and national government, trusts and foundations – should look at ways of engaging young people in society in innovative ways. This report has demonstrated not only the need for greater investment in young people, but also the great potential for young people to give something back.

Conclusions

The findings indicate that there is much to be learned from young people's view of 'charity', and from how they see their own role in civil society and their relationship with charities now and in the future.

Widening our understanding of charitable giving means recognising that young people do a lot more than they are sometimes given credit for in society, and celebrating this fact. We also need to provide more (and different) opportunities for young people to become engaged with forms of citizenship and building social capital. It is vital for the charity, voluntary and community sector to address young people's concerns, as the future of the sector and the shape of civil society will depend on the input of today's young people.

Introduction

The facts about young people's giving and participation

Various recent research studies have shown evidence of a decline in charitable activity among young people, both in terms of volunteering and giving. Figures show that 43 per cent of 18–24 year olds volunteered an average of 0.7 hours per week in 1997, compared with 55 per cent of this age band volunteering 2.7 hours in 1991 (Davis Smith, 1997). The 16–24 age band is the population group least likely to give money to charity (Jas, 2002), with just over half (55 per cent) contributing in 2000 (compared with 72 per cent of 25–34 year olds). Age has long been considered an important determinant of giving, and the Institute of Fiscal Studies (IFS) has calculated that, for every 10-year increase in the age of the head of a household, there is a 3 per cent increase in the likelihood of giving (Banks & Tanner, 1997). The IFS research has, however, also shown a generational effect over the last two decades, with those with a head of household in their twenties being significantly less likely to give than the previous generation of their age.

Some have seen the decline as part of a general trend towards social disaffection in this age group. Alongside the decline in giving, it has been claimed that participation rates in the last election, in which six out of ten of 18 to 25 year olds did not vote, 'showed the strength of political disaffection among young people' (Walker, 2001). The two main political parties have disproportionately small and declining youth memberships (Ward, 2002; Wintour, 2002), and young people are the least likely of any age group to attend a religious group.

This is a concern to many for whom engagement in the community is fundamental to a civilised society. The government and the general public alike have expressed the need for strong civil societies, in which people play an active part as stakeholders, particularly through the many voluntary activities and associations in which they are engaged. Levels of giving to voluntary associations – whether of time or money – can therefore be seen as a key social indicator of public spiritedness, generosity, social responsibility, and of the existence of social capital (Putnam, 1995).

On a more positive note, the 1995 British Social Attitudes (BSA) survey showed that young people placed a higher priority on their charitable giving than older people did, and they gave greater importance to the role of the voluntary sector in dealing with social problems (Pharoah, 1997). Young people aged 16–24 give an average of £6.99 per month; the average for the whole population is £11.82 (Jas *et al.*, 2002).

For some causes and needs, younger people may favour alternative, more radical solutions, believing, for example, that ethical trading (i.e. buying fairly traded products) benefits developing countries more than charitable giving (NOP, 1994). The 1993 BSA survey also showed that younger people (and those with lower incomes) were more likely to agree that the government should provide more for needs rather than relying on charities to do so. In general, younger people (and those on lower incomes) were also less likely to agree that people should look after themselves and not rely on charities. Young people seem to hold the most idealistic and least critical views of charities and are the age group least likely to consider them wasteful or out of touch.

Young people's relationship with charities, volunteering and giving

If there is a generational turn away from affinity with society and the concept of an active community, then perhaps the charitable sector should try to understand why this is happening and to rekindle the involvement of young people.

VOLUNTEERING AND PARTICIPATION

As noted in the previous section, the decline in charitable giving among young people has been accompanied by a decline in young people's participation in volunteering, as shown in research by the IVR (Davis Smith, 1999). Many of the studies on young people's participation in voluntary work have uncovered that the image of the charitable sector may be an issue with young people: 41 per cent thought that their friends would regard volunteering as 'uncool' (Davis Smith, ibid), and research by the National Centre for Volunteering showed the image of volunteering to be 'rigid' and 'worthy' (McCurry, 2000).

A recent survey by the Guide Association on citizenship found that 'the enthusiasm [for effecting social change] of 9–10 year olds has often all but disappeared by the time they reach the ages of 15 or 16' (Guide Association, 2001). This decline in enthusiasm is more profound for young people from lower socio-economic backgrounds, who feel consistently more disengaged and disempowered. The report notes a transition period from ease to effort in joining in communal activities, and at all ages small immediate actions are easier than longer-term or more difficult or costly involvement: '[T]here is a definite gap between saying they would like to be more involved and actively following this up. This may be due to lack of information on how to go about it or a more general apathy' (Guide Association, ibid). The Guide report notes a high level of charitable activity but that this is mainly organised through schools.

Eight per cent of students who take gap years use the year to volunteer, but, according to the National Centre for Volunteering (Ramrayka, 2001), most charities have not targeted 'gappers' enough. Justin Davis Smith of the IVR therefore interprets the decline as 'not so much a decline in altruism as a failure of … organisations to move with the times' (Davis Smith, 1999).

It is also a time when many young people fall through the gaps in formal organised social structures, and when their lives are no longer structured by external bodies, such as school, which may actively require participation in social and community activities like sports, Scouts or Guides.

Perhaps young people should not be judged solely on their financial contributions: although only 3 per cent of Oxfam's regular donors are aged 18–24, 13 per cent of their campaigners are in this age group (Ashdown Group, 2001), and the average age of a donor to Greenpeace (at the radical end of the charity spectrum) is 30 (Anderson, 2001). Lord Irvine recently lamented the 'worrying trend' that young people are interested in direct action and single issues (White, 1998), but charities are very often 'single issue' groups (e.g. environment, poverty, homelessness, etc). The participation of many young people in huge numbers at anti-capitalism marches, anti-war marches, and in the riots in the North of England last year shows that, although there may be dislocation, apathy may not be an accurate label.

GIVING

Young people are the least likely of all age groups to use planned giving methods such as covenant or direct debit (although advocates of face-to-face street fundraising methods suggest that this age group is the most likely to sign up for direct debits currently, there are no published figures to back this up) or tax-effective methods such as Gift Aid or payroll giving (CAF/IR/NCVO, 1999), tending instead to give in more spontaneous and sporadic ways such as pub collections and sponsorship (Pharoah, 1997). This may be explained by the fact that one-quarter of 16–25 year olds do not have a bank account (Guardian Unlimited, 2001). Maybe some of the fundraising methods that charities use inadvertently exclude some young people. Yet this does not necessarily mean that young people will not become engaged in future. One study found that 16–24 year olds were the most likely age group to say that they are likely to use tax-effective methods of giving in future (CAF/IR/NCVO, 1999). It has also recently been reported that, since the tax changes introduced in April 2000 made Gift Aid accessible to all and raised the profile of giving to charity, more young people are being attracted to give for the first time (Walker *et al.*, 2002).

In light of young people's comparatively limited spending power, it is understandable that charities tend not to direct a large proportion of their limited fundraising budget at young people specifically. The majority of charitable income comes from middle-aged people (aged 35–55), and charities have aimed their fundraising at these groups; some have also concentrated on direct debits, Gift Aid and payroll giving. Only 1 per cent of young people give through direct debit (Pharoah, 1997); many are not taxpayers; one-quarter do not even have a current account.[1] As Cathy Pharoah (ibid) has explained, 'the pressure for cost-effective fundraising means campaigns explicitly target middle-aged, middle class groups to the exclusion of others.'

It may also be that the generosity of young people is under-reported: many give through schools, colleges, universities and workplaces – and this may fall below the radar of conventional survey methods. Many young people may also give through their parents. Indeed, an additional factor to consider is 'pester power' – according to recent surveys, young people today exert more pressure on their parents and wield more influence in family economic decision making. A survey by the Abbey National, for example, found that more than half of youngsters living at home had the final say on many household spending decisions (Bowers, 2000). Similarly, in a national survey of giving, 24 per cent of adults said they discussed their charitable donations with their children (Walker *et al.*, 2002), and households with children are 3 per cent more likely to give to charity than those without (Pharoah, 2002a). This may mean that the influence exerted by young people on their elders provokes greater charitable giving (a benevolent 'pester power') – and one could argue that this money should be attributed to the influential young.

A further possibility is that many young people simply do not have what they feel is adequate income at this stage in their lives to support charitable giving, but they intend to in future. This hypothesis of the economic life cycle proposes that people of this age group will tend to spend more than they earn and not have any spare disposable income for behaviour such as saving or giving until they reach their thirties. On the other hand, it is in this age band (16–24) that most young people leave education and enter the world of work – the first time many of them will have earned disposable income and the freedom to choose how to use it. The majority of individuals in this age group will have no dependents and fewer economic ties.

Those young people with disposable incomes are more likely to visit night-clubs, cinemas, public houses, sports centres and fast-food restaurants – areas in which charities have not traditionally advertised. This may be one of the reasons why many young people feel that charities have less relevance to their own experience. It is clear that they believe that charity advertisements should give more feedback about how money is used, and that information should be made more relevant and exciting to them (CAF/IR/NCVO, 1999).

---

1 Mintel research, quoted in *Guardian Unlimited*, Money, 2001.

Social change

The last two decades have witnessed considerable social change in the UK, which is likely to have had various impacts on young people's behaviour and life experiences.

This is the generation (broadly speaking, those under 30) that has grown up in and after the era of Thatcher. Society as a whole, so one argument goes, has become more individualised: all age groups are less likely to vote, to go to Church, and to give to charity than they were 20 years ago, but the trend is most pronounced among the under 30s, who are also less likely to volunteer (Davis Smith, 1997; CAF/IFS, 2000). Opinion is divided as to whether this is the effect of a specific cohort or whether it represents an increasing tendency for the young not to give.

INEQUALITY

Young people suffer from the polarisation of wealth seen in society as a whole over the last two decades. Some have been disadvantaged by the effects of successive governments' withdrawal of benefits and student grants paid to young people.

The picture is worse for those of a lower socio-economic status. According to a 1998 report by the Department of Environment, Transport and the Regions (DETR), 'for young people (16–24), the state spends on average 14 per cent less money on young people in deprived areas, than on the average young person' (DETR, 1998). While the 1980s saw overall living standards rise, the 'numbers of people living in, or on the margins of, poverty increased dramatically' (Giddens, 1997), with 'an unmistakable trend towards sharply rising child poverty' (Kumar, 1993).

CRIME

Total recorded crime doubled between 1980 and 1993 (*The Economist*, 1997), and young people in the 16–24 age group are the group most likely to commit a crime. They are also the group most likely to be a victim of crime. In the UK 'one in six 16 to 24 year olds are the victim of a violent offence each year', the highest figure in Europe (Graham & Bowling, 1995).

GLOBALISATION AND THE LABOUR MARKET

The labour market in the UK has changed extensively over the past 20 years. There has been a massive decline not only in manufacturing, but also in the notion of a 'job for life'. The labour market is increasingly competitive and jobs more insecure, although overall unemployment has fallen since its mid-1980s peak.

This may be influencing young people's perceptions and their expectations in relation to financial security. At the same time, more young people than ever have been given the opportunity to attend further and higher education as they seek to gain advantage in the labour market, a development which in turn is putting a strain on college resources, and on young people's finances. Higher expectations are being raised while the labour market is increasingly insecure. Other factors are changing the life pattern of this generation – for example, the fact that young people are living at home longer, marrying later, and finding it less easy to buy property as a result of the spiralling costs of first homes.[2]

YOUNG PEOPLE'S FINANCIAL SITUATION

Two separate pieces of research last year, by Abbey National and by the Co-operative Supermarket Chain, revealed the level of young people's influence on their parents' purchasing decisions (Bowers, 2000). Advertising agencies have long recognised the effect of so-called 'pester power' and branding, with the result that young people are one of the most brand-conscious groups, and one that is the target of considerable marketing activity. Young people also tend to have a strong desire to spend their money on themselves, especially when disposable income is still a novelty (CAF/IR/NCVO, 1999). As Naomi Klein (2000) points out, young people now experience 'the tentacles of branding reaching into every crevice of youth culture … making the keeping-up-with-the-Joneses consumerism of their suburban parents pale by comparison.'

Rising consumer power and access to loan finance mean that 38 per cent of 17–22 year olds owe more than £1,500 (King, 2002). The steep rise in the housing market and the diminution of the state pension have also meant that, from an earlier age, there are greater pressures on young people's disposable income than has previously been the case.

Conclusions so far – taking a balanced view

We may be mistaking diversity for apathy when considering young people's engagement with the voluntary sector and giving. Research shows that the declines in charitable giving, volunteering, and electoral turnout are not restricted to young people but are true of the population as a whole. It may also be that young people are defining new issues or causes that are important to them, but to which the charitable sector has not responded; and that a more independent generation finds no appeal in putting change in a collection tin or volunteering in a shop. For instance, charity challenge holidays (e.g. cycling 450km around Laos) entice 'a high number of young people, asomething many charities lack [the ability to do]'.[3] Have charities become too established, too mainstream, not radical enough?

This research aims to disentangle these diverse threads and to find out exactly what young people think about charity, the appropriateness of their involvement with charity and about giving to charity. Previous studies have suggested that younger people's engagement in voluntary associations or activity hinges on perceptions of appropriateness and

2 House prices have increased by 250 per cent since 1985 (*The Economist*, 1997; Willcocks, 2002), while wages have risen by just under 100 per cent in the same period (*The Economist*, 1997; ONS, 2001a).

3 Mark Astarita from the National Deaf Children's Society, quoted in Buckley, 2002.

relevance, and on there being adequate opportunities and information. The research presented here aims to develop our understanding of young people's giving to charity, to explore young people's perceptions of charity and to investigate the different ways in which they give to charity. In the process, it seeks answers to such questions as: Who do young people think should be responsible for charitable support? What are the causes they consider important? What are the factors that influence their giving?

If elements of society have ceased to engage with young people, the voluntary sector may also, as a result of its diversity, be very well placed to recapture the imagination of the disaffected and excluded members of this generation, and in the process to promote a more positive image of youth.

This research aims to provide necessary baseline information on young people's donating money to charities. The information will be invaluable to those involved in campaigning initiatives, to those involved in developing material for the new citizenship course in the school curriculum, to policy makers involved in designing a wide variety of programmes for young people, and to charities themselves, as they re-define their role and missions within changing social contexts for young people.

Methods

The research used both qualitative and quantitative methods. The aim was to allow young people to talk about charity and giving in a neutral setting and then to follow this up with benchmarking questions in a quantitative survey. Fieldwork for the study was carried out between March and June 2002.

FOCUS GROUPS

Nine focus groups were carried out with a total of 70 young people (in groups of 4–12 individuals). Variations in the groups were by: geographic location across the UK, setting (urban, semi-urban or rural), and social context (e.g. workplace, school or college, social activity group). Groups were also chosen to provide a rough balance of gender, age and ethnic profiles. Appendix 2 provides an account of these focus groups, and of their breakdown in terms of social context, geographical location, setting, age, gender and ethnic profile.

The majority of the focus groups were undertaken and analysed by the two authors, providing a balanced gender and age input (one of the authors was within the target age group of participants at the time of the research). Appendix 3 presents the topic guide the authors and others used with the focus groups. Three groups were facilitated by an independent consultant, Dr Katharine Gaskin, with whom the authors worked closely, and whose groups they attended as note takers. One of the groups was facilitated by the Centre for Ethnic Minority Studies (who organised the Islamic Society group at Royal Holloway University) in the belief that an 'insider' would be better for the discussion, but again one of the authors was present to take notes and to ensure continuity.

NATIONAL SURVEY

A quantitative survey was carried out with a nationally representative probability sample of 590 young people aged 16–24. The survey was carried out by BMRB International using face-to-face CAPI interviews (Computer Assisted Personal Interviewing) in the ACCESS national omnibus, and was weighted according to gender, age, employment status of housewives (and whether they have children), social class and standard region. The quantitative survey questionnaire is presented in Appendix 4.

Young people's engagement with giving to charity

This section presents the findings of the two parts of the research project: the discussions of the focus groups and the results of the national survey. The responses to the questions asked in the focus groups are presented together with the survey results to give an overview of the main themes and opinions that emerged from the two stages of the research. The structure of this section approximately follows that of the topic guide used by the facilitators in the focus group sessions (see Appendix 3), and is divided into the themes below.

- **Perceptions of charity** looks at how young people define charity, what relevance they consider it to have and what role it plays in their lives today.

- **Giving to charity** covers the various ways in which young people currently engage with charities and their communities, how they give time, money and other resources; it also looks at whose responsibility they feel it is to give money, the causes they tend to support, and how young people perceive and react to marketing and fundraising efforts.

- **Relating to charities** looks at young people's relationships with charities, what they have and what they want, and finds out how much trust and confidence they have in charities' ability to fulfil their charitable purpose.

- **Future engagement** looks at how young people think they will engage with charity in the future, and at whether and how they will give money and time.

Attribution of quotes from the focus groups

Participants in the focus groups contributed anonymously: quotes are therefore attributed only to their group of origin, giving the type of group, geographic location and age range of participants. Some excerpts represent exchanges between group members, but most are comments of one individual within a group most representative of the group consensus on each issue.

Perceptions of charity

SUMMARY

Charity is not a topic at the forefront of young people's minds, and it is not the first thing they'd think to do with their money. When it is discussed, however, they have a well-developed sense of what charity is and what charities do, and view favourably charities' role in raising awareness, and helping people and situations. They define the concept of 'charity' more widely than formal organised charity activity, but still think the charity sector does more good in society than government or business, and have greater trust in it than in the other two sectors.

WHAT IS CHARITY?

At the beginning of this exploration of young people's perceptions of 'charity' it was important not to predefine the concept itself. This opening question was therefore left deliberately open so that the participants of the focus groups could define 'charity' in their own way, without limiting their thinking to formal charities, and discussions then followed up these definitions. It was clear from the transcripts, however, that, although young people seem to define the concept of 'charity' more widely than their older counterparts, many do not clearly differentiate in many contexts between charity as a concept (i.e. the act of being charitable) and charity as a collection of charitable organisations. This should be borne in mind throughout the analysis.

In the focus groups, the participants were first asked to write down their initial thoughts of what 'charity' was, and what they thought of when they heard the word 'charity'; each participant then read out their contribution. This was followed by a discussion in each group.

Most of the responses given in the focus groups focused on concepts of giving to or simply helping people who were in need, on the idea of charity as meaning the equivalent of 'the act of giving or helping':

> *Giving money, helping poor people in need.* (College, South-West, 16–19)

> *It's not just money; you can give things like clothes or time to help as well.* (University Christian Union, Scotland, 18–22)

> *Helping people out – but there's different types, like, some people do fundraising, you can buy things, or for other people it's just giving; you're not getting anything back.* (Employed, North England, 17–23)

> *Someone or some group that gives help to some other group for no personal gain.* (Employed, North England, 17–23)

About a quarter included in their concept of charity actual named charities, using charity to mean a body that does something charitable (see Appendix 1 for a list of the most named charities: 33 different charities were named in all – the five most named charities were Oxfam, Cancer Research UK, NSPCC, the *Big Issue*, and the RSPCA).

WHAT IS THE ROLE OF CHARITY?

In answering this question, young people chose to define 'charity' as 'charities' and they approached their definition of charities' role in four ways.

The role of charities as intermediary between donor and recipient

You've got the people who are needy and then you've got them who make everyone aware, and then there's us who give them the money, and they [charities] then distribute it to where it needs it. (Employed, North England, 17–23)

The role of charities in providing care and support

It's not just giving money, it's the support for people like the cancer people: they may have all the money in the world, but they don't know how to support a friend or a member of the family; it's the support or the knowledge that the charity can pass on to them as well, not just the money. (Employed, North England, 17–23)

Apart from the material good they can do, it's about giving people hope too, not just the people getting aid. (University Christian Union, Scotland, 18–22)

The role of charities in campaigning and awareness raising

Raising awareness by shocking people. (College, South-East, 17–18)

I think it can raise awareness, and maybe, if a child sees a poster, when you give to the charity, it goes towards awareness or to helping after they've had problems, it's not necessarily going to stop it, but it can help. (Employed, Wales, 19–24)

Sometimes money is useful, but sometimes you need to pressure the big government to do something for the Third World. (College, South-East, 17–18)

The role of charities filling the gaps left by government

Charities can help fill in the gaps where governments don't, where they're missing things like respite care, or on an international level to help distribute the money where the government is not interested. They can focus on issues in a way that state governments can't. (University Christian Union, Scotland, 18–22)

ARE CHARITIES STILL NECESSARY IN THE TWENTY-FIRST CENTURY? *SHOULD* THEY STILL BE NECESSARY IN OUR MODERN SOCIETY?

Most young people emphatically believe that we still do need charities, indeed that charities are more necessary than ever:

> *[Charities are] more important today with the lack of support from government.* (Employed, North-West, 19–24)

> *More so, I believe, because there's lots of sub-sections of society that are getting lesser and lesser; the rich are getting richer and richer as the poor are getting poorer and poorer. And there are people with more time on their hands.* (Employed, North England, 17–23)

The young people in this study were acutely aware of inequalities in society:

> *There's more problems in today's society and nowadays people have more disposable income that can be used in charities.* (College, South-West, 16–19)

Others interpreted the question, disarmingly, as if it were self-evident:

> *There shouldn't be a need for it [charity], but the fact there are charities shows there's a need for it.* (Employed, North-West, 19–24)

Are charities the answer?

It appears that young people are also generally optimistic about the impact that charity can have on need. This was corroborated by the findings of the survey that followed up the focus groups, in which only 28 per cent of 16–24 year olds agreed with the statement 'I don't believe giving to charity is the answer to society's problems', while 43 per cent disagreed. Bear in mind again that 'charity', here as throughout, does not necessarily mean 'charities', although in this context it seems likely to largely include them. The results of the survey back this picture up, with those who strongly agree (that giving to charity is not the answer to society's problems) giving less money than those who strongly disagree (41 per cent of those strongly agreeing gave nothing to charity in the month before the survey, compared with only 22 per cent of those strongly disagreeing; and only 14 per cent of those strongly agreeing gave more than £10, compared with 23 per cent of those strongly disagreeing). It is worth noting, however, that almost 60 per cent who strongly agree that giving to charity is not the answer still give, so, although charity may not be seen as the ultimate answer, it may still be perceived as a viable and valuable option.

DEFINING 'CHARITABLE BEHAVIOUR'

In the focus groups, vignettes were used to give four realistic examples of what could broadly be described as altruistic behaviour. Again the intention was not to predefine or to define too narrowly the concept of charity. These examples were chosen to explore differences in young people's attitudes to: formal and informal definitions of giving; giving locally and internationally; giving time and giving money; as well as to what sort of person might be expected to engage in each activity (i.e. someone like themselves or someone unlike themselves); and their attitude to the activity itself.

The vignettes were as follows:

- **Person A – 'Fairtrade'**[1]
  When A goes shopping she makes sure she only buys coffee and bananas which have the 'Fairtrade' mark, so that the farmers in developing countries get a fair price for their products, even though it costs her more to do so.

- **Person B – 'Religious giving'**
  When B goes to Church each week, he gives some money on the collection plate to help keep the Church running.

- **Person C – 'Regular automated giving'**
  C regularly gives money every month from her bank account to a well-known charity.

- **Person D – 'Neighbourliness'**
  D has a neighbour who is elderly and finds it difficult to get to the shops, so he does her shopping for her every week.

Although many of the focus group participants had not heard of Fairtrade before, they appeared to understand the concept once it had been explained to them, and seemed very positive about it. None of the examples given was seen as not being 'charitable behaviour', which is in keeping with the broad definition of 'charity' and 'giving' being explored in the study. Young people's responses to each of the four examples given in the focus groups are briefly examined below.

Person A – Fairtrade

The response to **Person A**, who buys Fairtrade goods, was favourable and the response below was representative of most groups:

> *I quite like the idea of A, although it's not something that I do.*
> (Employed, Wales, 19–24)

Some of the younger participants additionally explained:

> *I don't usually go shopping, so I don't really find out.* (College, South-West, 16–19)

The results of the survey confirmed these positions, showing that only 6 per cent of young people said they had bought a Fairtrade product

---

1 'Fairtrade' or fair trade goods are generally slightly more expensive than their counterparts, as more of the money paid for the product goes directly to the producer instead of to any intermediaries. For more on this concept, see the Fairtrade Foundation (www.fairtrade.org.uk).

in the last month. These people were five times as likely to be from social class AB.

Further discussion in the focus groups uncovered seemingly pragmatic advantages given by some of buying Fairtrade goods over giving money directly to a charity:

> *Quite a lot of people don't actually like charity, so Fairtrade would be a really good one because they're earning it, whereas C [who gives through regular automated giving] - they're just getting given it.* (College, South-East, 17–18)

> *You actually encourage them to do something, and they're learning a trade at the same time; some people are … not proud to take money, but they want to do something for the money they're getting, and it will give them a sense of achievement.* (Employed, North England, 17–23)

Person B – Religious giving

The motives of **Person B** provoked a bit more scepticism than those of the other examples. Some felt that the money would be spent on the Church, but others also felt that the money might be spent in the community. These extracts from a conversation in one group encompass many of the issues raised:

> *He's helping his own.*

> *He would benefit from that money, if he goes to Church every Sunday … get a comfier seat or something.*

> *It's good if they give it to the community or on a school.*

> *He's still benefiting from it more than the other ones, although I don't think that's a bad thing. That might encourage more people to give money in a way, because you see something being done yourself, whereas if you just send it to a charity … [sentence not finished]* (College, South-West, 16–19)

Some also expressed doubts about what the money might be used for, once given. This level of scepticism seems, in the current international political climate, less surprising than it might otherwise be.

> *Some churches I've heard I'm not sure what they do with their money; I've heard they invest it in the arms trade and that.* (Unemployed, London, 19–24)

> *Muslims give in mosques and it went to al-Qaida.* (Employed, North-West, 19–24)

Person C – Regular automated giving

Person C, who gives on a regular basis, perhaps through direct debit, was seen as 'good'. Not everyone thought this a very active way of engaging, however, as these extracts from a conversation in one group demonstrate:

It's a steady income for the charity; at least they know it's coming every month.

That person's not really making any effort.

You just fill out a standing order form and that's it really, just like another bill in a way, you make sure the money's in there for that month. (College, South-West, 16–19)

Some people saw the ease of giving through direct debit as positive:

You don't even notice it, you don't feel it, it becomes a habit – like brushing your teeth. (University Islamic Society, South-East, 19–21)

I still think direct debit giving is good; it's good that it's something people can do easily. The charity's getting the money; you're getting back that altruistic feeling. (University Christian Union, Scotland, 18–22)

The national survey results confirmed the impression that young people can see the value of regular giving: 78 per cent of young people agreed that 'giving a small amount each month is a good way to give to charity'. This compares with 64 per cent of 11–16 year olds, according to recent Giving Campaign research. The national survey for this report also showed that regular giving increases slightly with age (30 per cent of 20–24 year olds give regularly, compared with 25 per cent overall).

Person D – Neighbourliness

There was near-universal agreement in naming **Person D** as the most charitable and that the contribution of Person D was the most 'valuable'; these opinions reflect similar comments in every group:

It's a lot more personal, a lot more meaningful, rather than just if you've got wealth. (Employed, North England, 17–23)

In a way, I think D is more because they're putting the effort in and going out and actually doing something. (College, South-West, 16–19)

I think D, yeah, I give money by direct debit, but it's just one of these things that comes round, and that for me is a lot easier. It would be a lot harder for me to go out and do someone's shopping, but maybe it's easier for someone else. (Employed, Wales, 19–24)

So what was it about Person D that provoked such a universal response across the groups? It appears that the actions of Person D evoked some sense of society, of community cohesion, friendliness, and of what Robert Putnam would call 'social capital':

Time, it has more of an effect on the person you're giving time to. It's like the gentleman [in the vignette] doing the shopping each week: it takes his time, and she [the neighbour in the vignette] feels more safe in the area that they're in. (Employed, North England, 17–23)

> *It's one-to-one caring as well: if you put money on a plate or something, that's it, you've done it; but, if you do the shopping for somebody and then go back and have a cup of coffee, it's time and effort.* (College, South-West, 16–19)

> *You're getting to see the personal returns, you're getting to see them smile.* (University Christian Union, Scotland, 18–22)

The focus group participants were also asked to identify **what sort of person acts in charitable ways**. They were asked to describe the character of the person they might associate with each of the four activities described in the vignettes, and how they view the 'charitableness' of each activity. Their comments on each person are summarised below:

- **Person A** 'housewife', 'middle-aged with children', 'less well off', 'an eco-warrior', 'middle class', 'doesn't have that big an income', 'conscious of the world'

- **Person B** 'religious', 'godly', 'old', 'aged 55', 'coffin dodger'

- **Person C** 'middle-aged businesswoman', 'well off', 'businessman', 'someone working', 'office worker', 'quite rich'

- **Person D** 'middle-aged', 'kind', 'caring', 'housewife', 'a person with a good culture', 'helpful'

In terms of which activity young people think **most 'charitable'**, although Person D gained most support, the other common response came in the following form:

> *They're all equal. They're all giving something in the way they can, and that's all charitable.* (College, South-East, 17–18)

Some made a distinction not on the grounds of how money or help was given but on the motives behind giving or helping:

> *As a Muslim you have to look past [the amount given] … so to say who is more charitable would be the one who's got the most purest of intention.* (University Islamic Society, South-East, 19–21)

> *It would be better if they could have decent motives behind it, because, if they actually changed their motives, they might be more inclined to give more as well.* (University Christian Union, Scotland, 18–22)

Again, this suggests that young people define 'charity' and 'charitable behaviour' more widely than some more formal definitions. It is also worth noting that all of the four examples were seen as activities carried out by older, middle-aged or elderly characters. This may suggest that such charitable activities are something young people will do when they mature, but it also reveals the challenge inherent in developing images of charitable behaviour relevant to young people, in which they can identify themselves. The good news is that the characters and the activities were generally seen as positive.

Giving to charity

SUMMARY

Young people are engaged in various activities that could be described as broadly 'altruistic' or 'charitable', but which may not be counted under the more formal banner of 'charity' (including recycling, giving old goods to charity shops, giving to beggars and campaigning about issues). Young people perceive that many charities tend to concentrate on the monetary aspects of giving. They know that money is a crucial part of charity and feel that people should give to support charity. However, most young people feel that they haven't got much money, and feel that charities should try to get them involved in other ways e.g. giving old clothes, getting involved in events or helping out ('volunteering').

GIVING IT AWAY

As much of younger people's giving of money to charity is 'small change' giving, the research constructed a scenario to test out whether participants in the focus groups would think of giving to charity from a small windfall. They were asked whether they would give anything to charity from a £10 note if they found it unexpectedly in their bag or coat pocket.

The majority of respondents quite openly stated that charity would not be the first thought that entered their heads if they found the £10 in their own possession:

> *You think 'Oh great, I can treat myself', that is your immediate thought.* (Employed, Wales, 19–24)

Others thought they might be 'generous' with the money, rather than strictly charitable:

> *The closest you'd get to charity is spend it on your friends, buy them a drink or something.* (College, South-East, 17–18)

For other groups, their own situation may warrant a little charity itself:

> *We're students [followed by much laughter] … tenners are very few and far between.* (College, South-West, 16–19)

Charity was not at the forefront of their considerations, even if they found the money in the street:

> *It would depend on what was immediate; if there was someone collecting in the street then you might give it to them, but otherwise I'd probably keep it unless there was the opportunity.* (University Christian Union, Scotland, 18–22)

> *If you'd found it on the street and you'd just got a big phone bill that day, you'd be less likely to give it, I think; well, I would.* (University Christian Union, Scotland, 18–22)

Others also picked up on the need for something to prompt them to consider a charitable option:

> *You don't really think about it until you're asked and you see a collection going on.* (College, South-West, 16–19)

In a similar scenario, the survey revealed that 83 per cent of young people said that they would get involved if their college or employer organised a charity event. Young people are receptive to the idea of giving, but may respond best when prompted.

OTHER WAYS OF 'GIVING'

Participants in the focus groups were asked to name any other ways of 'giving' that they could think of, following the discussions around the vignettes mentioned above. They came up with a variety of different options with relative ease:

> *We gave shoeboxes with toothpaste and soap.* (College, South-West, 16–19)

> *Christmas boxes at high school – given to elderly.* (College, South-East, 17–18)

> *Giving something physical like clothes.* (College, South-West, 16–19)

> *Counselling for victims of domestic violence or racial attacks. That is part of charity because people can't afford to get help … women who got beat and that.* (Unemployed, London, 19–24)

> *The one about buying Fairtrade coffee [vignette Person A, above], the person doing that could also lobby government; that also could be a form of charity.* (University Islamic Society, South-East, 19–21)

> *Give research skills, computer skills, scientific skills, for the benefit of mankind.* (University Islamic Society, South-East, 19–21)

> *I sometimes put some money in an envelope.* (College, South-West, 16–19)

> *Better development of areas: if [people] are running around doing crime, build a centre for them where they can come and communicate with other people and get skills.* (Unemployed, London, 19–24)

> *Collections at a workplace or a supermarket.* (University Islamic Society, South-East, 19–21)

> *At work, we do fundraising events.* (Employed, Wales, 19–24)

> *I'd do a sponsored event, sporting; you can have a laugh.* (Employed, North-West, 19–24)

> *Physically helping a neighbour to decorate.* (University Islamic Society, South-East, 19–21)

> *Playing the Lottery.* (Employed, Wales, 19–24)

Again it is worth noting that young people seem to define 'giving' very widely as a range of diverse activities carried out either by individuals or charities. It is also worth commenting that active engagement features highly on this list, with few of the examples involving giving money directly to a charity.

How are young people engaged in 'giving'?

In the survey, a representative group of young people were asked what their participation was in a number of activities that had been mentioned in the focus group discussions. Although not all these activities would necessarily be described as 'charitable' in the strictest sense, they could broadly be described as 'good deeds' or 'active engagement'. Of these deeds, 83 per cent of young people participated in at least one of these activities 'in the last month' (see Table 1).

Patterns of engagement among young people mirrors that of the rest of the population, with females and older young people (20-24 years), and those in higher social classes, being slightly more likely to participate:

- 87 per cent of females participated, compared with 80 per cent of males

- 87 per cent of 16-19 year olds participated, compared with 80 per cent of 20-24 year olds

- 93 per cent of people from social class AB participated, compared with 73 per cent of people from social class DE.

Table 1 Percentage of young people engaging in 'charitable' activities in the last month before the survey, in order of popularity (%)

Activity engaged in	Proportion of 16–24 year olds engaging (%)
Sponsored someone else to do something for charity	37
Recycled used materials (e.g. glass, cans, paper, clothes)	32
Given any goods to be sold in a charity shop or jumble sale	29
Given any money to a charity spontaneously in the street	28
Given money to beggars in the street	26
Given any money to charity as part of a regular giving arrangement	25
Bought the *Big Issue*	20
Bought anything in a charity shop	19
Spent time doing something for a charity (e.g. volunteering, sponsored activity)	12
Bought any Fairtrade goods	6
Campaigned on an issue you feel strongly about	5
Given any money in direct response to a charity advert or appeal in the media	3
None of these	17

To group these into activities:

- 53 per cent did something charitable (campaigning, volunteering, recycling)

- 45 per cent gave money directly to a formal (registered) charity

- 35 per cent bought charitable goods (e.g. *Big Issue*, Fairtrade and charity shop)

- 77 per cent gave money in any way (including purchasing charitable goods, buying Fairtrade products, giving to beggars)

- 42 per cent did all three – buying, doing and giving.

These figures compare well with an Observer/YouGov survey of 11–21 year olds which found that 67 per cent of this age range have (ever) given money to charity and 46 per cent have (ever) done some voluntary work; and they compare well with research undertaken by the Giving Campaign, which found that 65 per cent of 11–16 year olds had given money to charity in the last six months – although, in both cases, as noted previously, loaded phrases such as 'voluntary work' and 'giving money to charity' should be used and interpreted with caution.

There were some notable, if unsurprising, gender and age differences in participation in the activities listed in the survey: females were more likely than males to give goods to and buy goods from charity shops, while males were more likely to give money to beggars in the street; older young people (20–24) were more likely than younger ones (16–19) to buy in a charity shop and to give regularly. Higher social classes were more likely than lower ones to participate in all activities except buying goods in a charity shop, which was highest among social classes DE and C2.

Table 2 How much young people gave to charity 'in the last month' (%)

Amount given	Proportion of young people giving that amount (%)
Nothing	23
<£1	10
£1–£4.99	31
£5–£9.99	18
£10–£49.99	13
£50+	2

The average amount given by young people in the last month before the survey was £6.94, although the modal amount was slightly lower – between £1.00 and £5.00 (see Table 2). This figure is almost identical to the figure of £6.99 in the national data collected by NCVO/NOP and compares with an average for the whole population of £11.82 (Jas *et al.*, 2002). This suggests that, when you take into account their relative incomes, young people appear comparatively generous. Young people tend to give to charities either regularly or spontaneously, with only around one-third doing both in the last month before the survey.

This all suggests that young people are firmly engaged in giving money as well as in buying charitably and in performing 'charitable' activities. They are most likely to be involved in activity-based giving (e.g. sponsorship) and are more likely to get engaged in a 'charitable' or community-minded activity than to give money direct to a charity.

It is interesting to note that, if such informal methods of giving money to 'charity' as giving to beggars, buying in charity shops and buying Fairtrade goods are included in the figures, the percentage of young people giving shoots up to 77 per cent.

These figures might also provide some encouragement to those charities with shops, since they show that these are an important point of contact with young people.

As other research has also shown, campaigning is another relatively popular activity for this age group. For example, the Face Youth Census 2002 found that 25 per cent of young people had been on a protest march, and research by the Guide Association found that 46 per cent of 15–24 year olds had signed a petition. It is interesting to note that analysis of the survey shows that those that do participate in campaigning activities are also more likely to give more money to charity.

This pattern, of course, reflects the choices presented to young people in the question but may also say something about the opportunities for engagement they are presented with. Discussions in the focus groups brought up the issue of charities that are seen to focus too much of their effort on raising money from young people and not enough on getting them involved and persuading them to give time or other resources. In the survey, only a minority of respondents (19 per cent) felt that there were not enough opportunities for them to give money to charity, while 42 per cent of young people felt that there were not enough opportunities to give time to charity. Time was regarded in the focus group discussions as an important commodity to give to charity – as important, in many cases, as giving money (the survey found that 26 per cent of young people agreed that they would prefer to give time to charity than to give money; 32 per cent disagreed). This may be a preference that shifts with age, since the Giving Campaign research of 11–16 year olds found that 41 per cent preferred to give money, 16 per cent time, and that 43 per cent had no preference.

> *It's better for people of our age and maybe old people [to give time] – you've got time, maybe not enough money. People who are 30 or 40 might have a family and so maybe giving money is better for them.* (College, South-East, 17–18)

> *I think it's more important just to give.* (Employed, North England, 17–23)

Whose responsibility is it to give money to charity?

SUMMARY

In general, young people think that giving is the responsibility of everyone, although there was some debate about whether this is a duty or personal choice. But there was a feeling that those with more – wealthy people, government, companies – should perhaps give more, although opinion was rather split on the issue of relative responsibility. Age is not necessarily a factor, and the vast majority of those surveyed thought that younger people have just as much responsibility to give as older people.

A DUTY TO CARE?

There was much spontaneous discussion in the focus groups about whether 'responsibility' to give implies duty or choice. Strong views were expressed on both sides, and this perceptual division continues in the ensuing sections.

> *It's more choice … I think personally if you can give, you should; it's just human, just humane, whether you give time or whatever.* (Employed, North England, 17–23)

> *Duty in some ways, because I have way more than I need, so it's my duty to give up some of it, because I don't need it.* (University Christian Union, Scotland, 18–22)

> *It's a choice. I do wish more people would give, because I give, but none of my friends give.* (Employed, Wales, 19–24)

> *I didn't do anything to be born in this position in Europe, with money. I got a gift and so I feel like I have a duty: I was lucky, and you think 'What if I was born in Africa and not in Europe?' I was lucky; it's my duty.* (College, South-East, 17–18)

The young people in the focus groups had different opinions about who – the rich, the government, older people or young people – had more responsibility to give.

RICHER PEOPLE'S RESPONSIBILITY

Young people emphasised their own relative poverty as a reason for not giving most strongly when talking about richer people, whom they therefore considered to have a greater responsibility to give to charity than they did. In this regard, at least some thought that responsibility came with riches:

> *Charity, it's not my concern; the big chairmen've got millions of pounds.* (Employed, North-West, 19–24)

> *It's easier for them.* (Employed, Wales, 19–24)

> *I think it's the responsibility of the rich to give more … because they have more, and because they probably made it off someone who has less, and potentially as a result of their actions. If you've made a lot from the community doing whatever then you have a responsibility to give back.* (University Christian Union, Scotland, 18–22)

> *I don't think it's anyone's responsibility to; it's your choice. But I just wish it was more people's choices to give more – but maybe people who have got more should give more.* (Employed, Wales, 19–24)

A few, however, believed that the motivation for giving was more important, and simply giving money is not enough:

> *It's got to be from somebody who really wants to make a difference and really cares.* (College, South-West, 16–19)

Bigger responsibility if you've got more; but you have to believe in it. (Employed, North-West, 19–24)

Although it seemed the majority view in the focus group discussions, the survey found that fewer young people (37 per cent) agreed with the statement that rich people had more responsibility to give to charity than they did, while 42 per cent disagreed. This may illustrate the strong belief that it is everyone's responsibility to give, as the previous section indicated.

GOVERNMENT'S RESPONSIBILITY

Opinion was divided on the role of government, although the tone was generally negative about the government's perceived effectiveness:

They can't run the country, let alone doing stuff for other people. (Employed, North England, 17–23)

It's not central government, [although] they should be more effective; the essence of charity is individuals giving to what they believe in. (Employed, North-West, 19–24)

Others hinted at a lack of appropriate priorities:

Wouldn't it be great if schools and hospitals had all the money they needed and armies had to hold jumble sales to raise money? (University Christian Union, Scotland, 18–22)

For the environment, the government should tax private chemical companies. (Employed, North-West, 19–24)

The government … they get our tax: we pay to the police to protect, they should give money to the poor to protect them. We need to give as well, but the main role is the government for welfare. (University Christian Union, Scotland, 18–22)

The demarcation between the government's responsibility and the role of charities was hotly debated. Many young people had clear views on what the government should take responsibility for:

There are some things that it seems it makes much more sense for the government to fund; things like Bible distribution or art charities are much more appropriate for personal giving than things like international development, which are a government purpose. (University Christian Union, Scotland, 18–22)

I wouldn't actually class books for schools or computers for schools as charity, because it should actually come from the government. (Employed, Wales, 19–24)

Others thought that there was less of a demarcation of boundaries and more of a blurred line between the government's obligations and responsibilities in terms of public spending and charities' obligations and responsibilities in terms of public fundraising:

I think the government has a responsibility in various areas, providing a level of social care, but charity is on top of that; but then governments will sometimes work through charities to achieve that. (University Christian Union, Scotland, 18–22)

We should all, collectively, try and improve people's situation … not just rely on our government. (University Islamic Society, South-East, 19–21)

If charities are just coming in behind where the government is failing at something, then should we really be addressing that the government is failing in a way and not pumping all our resources into charity provision? (University Christian Union, Scotland, 18–22)

That doesn't mean you shouldn't give to the charity, but in a way if you're creating a safety net … the government can think actually we can cut down our budget for this because they'll fill the gaps. (University Christian Union, Scotland, 18–22)

Third World poverty will never be solved by giving to charity; it needs governments. (Employed, North-West, 19–24)

Sometimes money is useful, but sometimes you need to pressure the big government to do something for the Third World. (College, South-East, 17–18)

Such views echo older adults' opinions about the role of government.

There was occasional confusion between the government and other large national ventures such as the National Lottery and the Millennium Dome, which provoked a great deal of criticism:

The government should give more, and the National Lottery gives it to theatres. (Unemployed, London, 19–24)

One thing that annoys me is the emphasis that went on the National Lottery when it was established, that it would give to charity, and the charities are just so not what I would consider charities at all. (University Christian Union, Scotland, 18–22)

I don't know if you've read in the newspapers the breakdown of what the Millennium Dome could have been spent on around the world, but it's ridiculous. (Employed, North England, 17–23)

YOUNG PEOPLE'S RESPONSIBILITY

In the survey, age was not seen as a factor in the responsibility to give: three-quarters of 16–24 year olds (74 per cent) agreed that 'people of my age have just as much responsibility to give to charity as older people' (13 per cent disagreed). This does not reflect the broad range of views expressed in the focus groups on this topic, however.

Some young people felt that their own financial situation imposed limits on their and their peers' giving, with 42 per cent of 16–24 year olds agreeing with the statement 'I don't have enough money to give to charity', although a similar proportion (38 per cent) disagreed. The

Giving Campaign's research found a similar proportion of 11–16 year olds believed they do not have enough spare cash to give to charity. In the focus groups, such comments were frequent:

> *I think it's equally important whatever age; it's just that people of our age at colleges and universities have got so many other money troubles that charity isn't one of their top priorities.* (College, South-West, 16–19)

> *I literally haven't got any money.* (College, South-West, 16–19)

> *If you've been to uni[versity], you're in debt; if you've not been to uni[versity] then you're not earning enough [to give].* (Employed, North-West, 19–24)

> *I don't think you can afford to do it [give money to charity], because you've got to save up to go to university; you can't afford every month, even though it is only £2, but when you're £12,000 in debt after university it's quite a lot to be giving that amount.* (College, South-East, 17–18)

> *Having an allowance off my parents, I don't feel it's my decision to give their money away. I mean, we tend to support the same charities, but it's not fair to.* (University Christian Union, Scotland, 18–22)

This may, of course, illustrate more about young people's priorities than the actual 'affordability' of giving, as some focus group participants acknowledged:

> *I think 'Oh I can only afford this much this week', but I know, if I thought about it, I could probably afford more; it's an obligation, because I'm lucky.* (University Christian Union, Scotland, 18–22)

> *Anything's better than nothing – any spare money at the end of the week should go to charity.* (Unemployed, London, 19–24)

A further factor that may discourage young people from giving was the perception that smaller gifts of money would not 'do as much good' as bigger gifts:

> *I could only afford to give coppers or maybe I could give £5, but then I think '£5, what's that going to do?' So that might deter me from doing it, because my money isn't going to do much. I know they say every little helps, but …* (University Christian Union, Scotland, 18–22)

Others pointed out that giving did not necessarily have to mean money and that being cash-poor did not necessarily mean you could not contribute anything:

> *Just by helping other people you can be charitable.* (College, South-East, 17–18)

> *There are things that students can give that people working in a 9-5 job can't, like we can go and volunteer much more easily.* (University Christian Union, Scotland, 18–22)

> *Everyone can help in their own way, as we've seen from that list [the vignettes]. Person D [helping with neighbour's shopping] didn't spend any money, and they still managed to help in a big way.* (College, South-West, 16–19)

Concern was voiced, however, over the perception that some charities appear to value gifts of money over gifts of time:

> *People don't advertise for your time as much as your money.* (College, South-East, 17–18)

> *I think if you really wanted to get involved you'd enquire yourself, cause they don't advertise. (College, South-East, 17–18)*

At the opposite extreme, a small minority voiced the opinion that young people have fewer responsibilities at their age, giving included:

> *It's all very much spend, enjoy, go out for meals, because you won't have a chance when you are older. There is less economic responsibility.* (University Islamic Society, South-East, 19–21)

What causes do young people prefer to support?

SUMMARY

The most important causes for young people are people-based: children, medical research and care, and aid for developing countries. Causes to do with animals and homeless people divide opinions. Young people will give equally to international causes and local ones, but they have less confidence in long-distance charity, as they can't see the good they do for themselves. Compared with an adult population, they rate homeless people, education and young people's causes higher, and heritage and museums and religious causes lower.

Given that young people perceive that they have less to give to charity in monetary terms, it is not surprising that they have strong priorities for their charitable money: some quite forceful views were expressed in this section.

WHAT CAUSES ARE IMPORTANT TO YOUNG PEOPLE?

There arc a plethora of charitable causes, not to mention multiple charities to respond to each of these causes. Yet young people generally found it easy to prioritise between the different charitable causes, and were confident in giving their reasons for their preferences. Favouring one cause, however, did not mean that no other causes were important, and some found it difficult to have to say 'No' to some charities (Appendix 1 gives a list of all the causes and charities named by the participants).

> *There is a limit to what you can do, though; it just seems to go on and on. You could give to absolutely everything, so*

sometimes you've got to be a bit horrible and say 'No'.
(University Christian Union, Scotland, 18–22)

Personal prioritising of the causes was felt to be necessary:

I don't think there should be much money spent on that [heritage]. I think there's other things it could be better spent on, but they could still have it in moderation, some money. (College, South-West, 16–19)

If there were no other problems [then participant would contribute to drug user rehabilitation], but they're last on the list … doesn't mean they're not important, but there are more important things. (Employed, North-West, 19–24)

Some of the focus group participants certainly felt that there were too many charities to choose from:

Too many small charities; you need one big organisation, not the little ones. (Employed, North England, 17–23)

When I heard there were 600 charities I just thought 'That's unbelievable; why don't they just all work together?'[2] (Employed, Wales, 19–24)

Prioritisation may also depend on circumstances, for example the availability of funds to give:

I would give to a charity that is helping to meet basic needs. I would choose that as opposed to medical research if I just had a small amount to give. (University Christian Union, Scotland, 18–22)

I think environmental and animal charities are much more ones that I'd give to on a one-off occasion when I get approached in the street, but long-term giving I would go for human interest charities. (University Christian Union, Scotland, 18–22)

PEOPLE FIRST

Human interest seemed to be the determining factor in most decision making, and 'people causes' certainly topped the list of most young people in the focus groups:

Personally, I would rather give to one that benefits people rather than animals. I'd probably give it to the NSPCC, not the RSPCA, because I feel I'd rather help a child in a council house than a dog in a council house. (Employed, North England, 17–23)

More things that are more important than that [the Arts], even the development of sport is more important than the Theatre or the Opera … keeps you fit, and countries that need money for aid and with AIDS [are more important]. (College, South-East, 17–18)

---

2 There are 185,948 charities on the Charity Commission Register for England and Wales (Charity Commission, 2002).

Top causes

In line with the general public, young people seem to give priority to medical care and research, with children's charities and international aid next in line. This seemed largely to follow personal experience or possible experience:

> *Cancer research, but not animals, and not so much the homeless because perhaps I won't be there in that situation.* (College, South-West, 16–19)

> *Things that have directly affected your family, like cancer research.* (College, South-East, 17–18)

The survey confirmed the findings of the focus groups, as the same three causes dominated young people's charitable thinking in terms of importance (see Table 3).

Table 3 Charitable causes considered most important by young people (%)

Cause	Proportion of young people rating as most important (%)
Medical research and/or care	35
Children or young people	19
Developing countries/Overseas aid	17
Homeless people in this country	7
Disabled people	6
Animals	5
Education	3
Elderly people	2
The environment	2
Museums, music, art, etc.	1
Religious causes	<1
Heritage	0

DOES CHARITY BEGIN AT HOME?

Do young people believe the old cliché that 'charity begins at home'? When they give, do they think of giving first to their local community, or do they think nationally or internationally? The focus groups provided a variety of views.

Some of the young people in the groups felt that charitable giving was important, but that their own immediate needs came first. Some, however, also recognised that the 'charity begins at home' cliché might be used to justify miserliness:

> *Generally an excuse not to give to charity … [but] you don't give 90 per cent of your wage to charity and then your wife and*

kids can't eat; things need to be kept in proportion. (University Islamic Society, South-East, 19–21)

Without doubt, you've always got to look after yourself: there's no point giving the shirt off your back to somebody else; you've got to make sure you've got enough to go around first of all. (Employed, North England, 17–23)

I don't know, I think a lot of people have said that to me, but, I don't know, I certainly don't think that. (Employed, Wales, 19–24)

Many young people drew a distinction between the relative need of people closer to home (in the community or in the UK) and the perhaps more urgent needs of those elsewhere (especially abroad):

Maybe it depends on how well-off you are yourself, sometimes, not necessarily as individuals; as a whole, as a country, we're better off than we've ever been. (Employed, Wales, 19–24)

To help someone in their neighbourhood maybe, like doing the shopping or cutting the grass for someone who is elderly or can't. But you can't just do that, you have to look further as well. If everyone did that, no one would give to the outside charities, abroad. (College, South-East, 17–18)

If you look out in the world there are people in a lot more need than everyone here; therefore, I would give to them because they are in more need. (University Islamic Society, South-East, 19–21)

Others saw needs in the UK as equally important, and this prompted some debate, as the following exchange illustrates:

It's not just abroad, it's over here that people haven't got much.

People abroad are poorer than in this country – no one is that badly off here.

To both, because both need it. Africa needs it, and our part of the world needs it. (College, Midlands, 16–18)

Responding to fundraising

SUMMARY

Several charity marketing and fundraising methods appear either to slightly annoy young people or to affect them too little to stimulate giving. Advertisements, sponsored activities and big charity events are more popular than face-to-face collections, celebrity or business endorsements. The survey found that, contrary to some beliefs, nearly two-thirds of young people seem put off by face-to-face fundraising methods – finding them intrusive and guilt-inducing – and they do not discriminate between beggars and charity collectors. Over three-quarters do, however, like the idea of giving a small regular monthly amount by direct debit. Celebrities' involvement in charity fundraising is viewed ambivalently, but it is not something that would greatly encourage young people to give, and they are wary of some celebrities 'just doing it for the publicity'. The younger respondents were more likely to be influenced by celebrities than those who were slightly older.

Charities employ various methods to fundraise. Which of these are most effective with young people? And do they inform or annoy, provoke giving or indifference?

FACE-TO-FACE FUNDRAISING[3]

There was an overwhelmingly negative opinion of all varieties of street collection, which was seen in the same light as other street 'selling' (from double-glazing salesmen to beggars and charity collectors). Most of the criticism focused on the intrusiveness of those collecting:

> *It's an invasion of privacy.* (Unemployed, London, 19–24)

> *I tar them all with the same brush as sales, better sent or e-mailed.* (Employed, North-West, 19–24)

The guilt factor was also an issue: just as there may be a 'warm glow' effect when you do give, there may be a 'cold shiver' effect when you are unable or unwilling.

> *A lot try and push people, and guilt people into doing it.* (Employed, North-West, 19–24)

Some certainly felt that there is an over-saturation of street collectors on the streets in many of the UK's towns and cities.

> *It's more like they're trying to tell you 'Give us your money', and put you in a position where, if you don't give or you can't give, you feel bad. Because I just don't, because if you walk down the main street ... on a Saturday afternoon you'll see four or five trying to sign you up for something or shaking a tin.* (Employed, Wales, 19–24)

There was widespread mistrust of many street collectors, which may partly stem from identification with others forms of 'begging'. For example, three young people recounted personal experience of having seen a street beggar 'hopping around the corner and getting in his BMW', or some similar incident.

Street collection is the most common method of everyday charitable giving (Walker *et al.*, 2002), but 60 per cent of young people in the survey said they did not like being approached in the street to give money, confirming the view given in focus groups. The survey also showed, however, that over one-quarter had given to someone 'collecting' on the streets 'in the last month'. They may find it harder than adults to say 'No' (the Giving Campaign research found that 69 per cent of 11–16 year olds feel guilty if they don't give money to charity when asked), although, in a survey of the general public, 57 per cent stated 'I can't refuse when someone comes to the door or approaches me in the street with a collecting tin' (Walker *et al.*, 2002).

---

3 This term is used to denote any form of personal fundraising, but particularly on the street, including the new face-to-face bib-wearing fundraisers who aim to sign people up using direct debit.

ADVERTISING

Generally, young people take the same kind of view about charity advertisements as the Independent Television Commission (ITC), which said, in its recent ruling on the NSPCC television advertisement of 'the child who doesn't bounce back' (featuring a cartoon child being knocked around by his father, bouncing back each time, but then turning into a real child at the end), that the advertisement was 'an effective means of communicating the seriousness of the issue'. This exchange was typical of many groups:

> *Some of them can be a bit nasty. Like Oxfam, you see little kids walking around carrying big buckets of water.*

> *Yeah, but they are showing the reality. They are saying 'Look, you are having a bath in your tub; he's having a bath in a bucket.'*

> *It's reality, really. To make you feel aware. There's no point pretending everything is happy dappy in the world, because it's not.* (Unemployed, London, 19–24)

And this opinion was widely held:

> *It makes you think, makes you feel sorry; yes, I would be more likely to give.* (College, West Midlands, 16–18)

Some, however, felt that appeals advertisements were a bit frustrating or irrelevant to them, since they felt unable to respond for a variety of reasons: for example, many young people cannot give over the phone, as they do not have credit cards. Nevertheless, many had reacted to appeals advertisements in other ways:

> *When we're this age it's hard to give because we don't have credit cards; you egg your Mum and Dad on to give.* (College, South-East, 17–18)

> *It's all very well us sitting here, but at the minute I wouldn't be able to do it ... but in five years' time, when I have more money, it's something I might think about.* (College, South-West, 16–19)

> *The adverts on TV don't actually make me give money, but, when I'm out on the street and they're collecting money, then ...* (College, South-West, 16–19)

Only 3 per cent of young people had given in direct response to a charity appeal or advertisement in the last month, according to the survey. This is partially explained by the need for a credit card to make a donation – the same applies to telethon appeals like Comic Relief and Children in Need. Despite the fact that many of them would not be able to participate in credit card appeals, 57 per cent agreed that charity advertisements or appeals make them more likely to give. This is perhaps a priming effect – next time they get the opportunity to give they may be more likely to give to the charity they have seen advertised. Young people also considered advertising an important general image raiser for charities: the survey found that 40 per cent agreed with the statement 'If I haven't heard of the charity before I won't give to them'. Appendix 1 shows that the majority of the charities named by young people are those that have a high-profile media presence.

CELEBRITIES

Young people thought that in some cases celebrities could add legitimacy to a particular cause or appeal, but some were suspicious about whether celebrities' motivations were genuine or not. Generally, however, cynicism was tempered by pragmatism:

> *A celebrity makes you think it must be all right, in a documentary.* (Employed, North-West, 19–24)

> *Some celebrities you can tell they really care, like Lenny Henry, and Bono – it's people who get involved rather than just give the money, go over to the country.* (College, South-East, 17–18)

> *It certainly could raise the profile of charities, but they probably do it to raise their own profile.* (University Christian Union, Scotland, 18–22)

The survey found that 45 per cent of 16–24 year olds said that they would not be influenced by celebrity involvement (only 28 per cent agreed that they would), and this was more pronounced in the older ages. Under one-quarter of 20–24 year olds said that celebrity endorsement would influence them to get involved. This rose to one-third of 16–19 year olds and, in Giving Campaign research, to 51 per cent of 11–16 year olds.

CORPORATE SPONSORSHIP

Some young people in the focus groups felt the same way about the role of companies sponsoring charities as they did about celebrity endorsement: it can be good for raising the profile of the charity but is best done with the perceived correct motivations.

> *They [companies] get a good press, but then you think of the amount you have to spend. But it's better than nothing at the end of the day, but then you think it's not that much if their sales are going to double – they should give more.* (Employed, Wales, 19–24)

SPONSORED EVENTS

When sponsoring a friend, young people's concerns about trust were more or less negated, which appeared to make them more likely to give:

> *You're not just giving to Joe Bloggs on the street; you're giving to someone who works in the same office as you.* (Employed, North England, 17–23)

The focus group discussions also raised the issue that taking part in sponsored events empowers young people to raise levels of money that they would otherwise be unable to, and may suit a perceived need for more active involvement:

> *I would certainly be inclined to, say, do something sponsored and raise that amount of money, because I personally wouldn't have that amount of money, but then if you go around getting 50p off people, then you feel like you've actually contributed something.* (University Christian Union, Scotland, 18–22)

The survey showed that in the last month 37 per cent of young people had sponsored someone to do something for charity (those in full-time or part-time employment were particularly likely to sponsor others).

CHARITY EVENTS

Events such as Comic Relief or Children in Need are also outlets for more active involvement in fundraising and giving, and were well-regarded among young people in the focus groups, as were the Blue Peter appeals:

> *They've got the hype so you get caught up in it.* (College, South-East, 17–18)

> *The beauty of that is that it is fun, they're not scared of like Lenny Henry going 'Give us your money'.* (Employed, Wales, 19–24)

> *If you're having fun, it's even easier to give to charity.* (College, South-East, 17–18)

> *We have fundraising here at college, and we give money at that.* (College, South-West, 16–19)

> *I think with Comic Relief they say £10 will buy you this amount of grain and you can see exactly what your money's going towards.* (Employed, Wales, 19–24)

A small minority raised a concern about the effect that such media-hyped fundraising might have on other, perhaps smaller, charities:

> *Somebody might think 'I've given £10 to Comic Relief, I don't need to give to any other charity that I see anywhere else', and so those that get all that limelight get everything.* (Employed, Wales, 19–24)

Relating to charities

SUMMARY

Young people want an active involvement with charities' work and they want to see and understand what charities do with their money. They seem to understand the constraints on what charities can do but, although they generally trust charities more than either the government or companies, young people have some concerns about charity spending. Young people want to see evidence that the money (especially their own money) has made a difference when given, and one-quarter cite knowing the money was spent well and made a difference as the thing most likely to make them give in the future. Overall, though, the vast majority (74 per cent) trusted charities to spend their money well.

WHAT KIND OF RELATIONSHIP DO YOUNG PEOPLE WANT WITH CHARITIES?

Active involvement

The findings have suggested that today's young people define charity more widely than formal organised charitable activities like giving money, and are more enthusiastic about engagement with 'giving' and 'charity' in terms of active involvement:

> *I think that young people have a different idea of charity from older people. I think for older people, I'm talking like late 50s, think of just giving money, but I think younger people would like to get more involved.* (Employed, Wales, 19–24)

> *I wouldn't want to be stood behind a counter in Oxfam waiting for someone to come in and buy a shirt or something; I'd rather be doing something.* (College, South-West, 16–19)

> *Actually I would like to know more about gap year – I would like more information.* (College, South-East, 17–18)

Some of the ways in which young people come into contact with charities are revealed in the survey.

In the last month:

- 29 per cent had donated something to a charity shop;

- 19 per cent had bought something in a charity shop;

- 12 per cent had given time either by volunteering or doing a sponsored activity;

- 5 per cent had campaigned on an issue about which they felt strongly.

One issue that was raised consistently in the focus groups was the perception that charities concentrate on the monetary aspects of charity, thus missing the opportunity for young people to become involved:

> *They advertise for your money, not your time. They don't want your moral side, just your cash.* (Employed, North-West, 19–24)

Only 19 per cent of young people felt there were not enough opportunities to give money to charity, but 42 per cent thought there were not enough opportunities to give time.

TELL US MORE

The young people in the focus groups also strongly expressed their need for more information from charities, not only about opportunities to get involved, but even more so about how they spend their donations and how this affects the needy recipients:

> *Charity groups should explain more what the money is for. I give money for undeveloped countries, but you can't actually realise what the money is used for - they should be clearer, and people would be more encouraged. That's why 'Children in Need' is good cause they show where they went last year to build a well or whatever, you think they are using the money well, and they've made their lives so much better.* (College, South-East, 17–18)

> *I want background information.* (Unemployed, London, 19–24)

> *Information before you give, and then an e-mail or a letter saying what your money went on.* (University Christian Union, Scotland, 18–22)

How can charities best communicate with young people? Almost half (47 per cent) of 11–16 year olds, according to the Giving Campaign, thought that charities should use the Internet more to get them interested, although this survey found that only 6 per cent of 16–24 year olds use the Internet to look up information on charities.

TRUST AND CONFIDENCE IN CHARITIES

The focus group discussions generally showed that charities are more trusted than either the government or companies, if only by default:

> *Businesses never do no good, and we don't really see what the government does.* (Employed, Wales, 19–24)

> *[I would trust] a handful of charities; the other two [government and business] are out of the question.* (University Islamic Society, South-East, 19–21)

In the focus groups there were some concerns voiced about the authenticity of some charities, although these were minority views:

> *There's was a documentary, might have been* Watchdog, *about people going around in London with badges saying 'We're collecting for whatever', but they never gave nowt to no one, they just counted it up and whatever they got went in their pockets.* (Employed, North England, 17–23)

Accountability was an issue central to young people in their relationship with charities. They had to trust the charity, and trust that it would make the best use of their money:

> *I wouldn't say that they were untrustworthy, but they might not be the most efficient with the money they've got.* (College, South-West, 16–19)

In research conducted by the Giving Campaign among the younger age group of 11–16, respondents thought that for every £1 they donated only 57p went on the charitable purpose (this compares with an average estimate of 44p – the modal was 50p for the whole population). Figures on charitable expenditure suggest that the figure for direct charitable expenditure is in fact around 81p in the pound (Pharoah, 2002b). The focus group discussions appear to show that 16–24 year olds may share the more pessimistic view.

> *Is there any director of a charity who isn't on a million pounds?*[4] (Employed, North-West, 19–24)

> *If you knew you'd be thinking how much goes into administration and running costs, I think it would put people off.* (Employed, Wales, 19–24)

> *Display how much goes to the bod, and we'd be less cynical.* (Employed, North-West, 19–24)

In fact, the survey found that 74 per cent of young people do trust charities to use their money well, with only 14 per cent distrusting them. Furthermore, it seems likely that those who distrusted could, with a little more information, be persuaded: the survey found that knowing that the charity spends the money effectively and makes a difference was cited by 25 per cent as the one thing that will make them give to charity in the future. Research by the Giving Campaign similarly shows that 76 per cent of 11–16 year olds trust charities to use donations wisely.

Overall young people were quite confident in charities' ability to effect change in a diverse range of situations. One of the most optimistic stated:

> *I don't think there's anywhere really where a charity couldn't make a difference.* (College, South-West, 16–19)

However, most felt that other important factors can constrain charities' abilities to effect change, chief among these being 'politics' and money:

> *Where politics come in, yeah … trade embargoes, war-torn regions, that's going to have an effect.* (Employed, North England, 17–23)

> *Governments undermine it with the arms trade, need it from a higher level – it's a political thing. You can't keep going and cleaning up the blood.* (Employed, North-West, 19–24)

> *I read an article on research, and that nowadays it is all about money, they are motivated by money. They might make a drug, which is expensive, it's a really good drug, and a similar drug could be made using cheaper material, but just as effective, but it is not made. The companies have laws which won't allow others to make these cheaper drugs, so it's all about money.* (University Islamic Society, South-East, 19–21)

4 It should be pointed out that there are no charity directors in the UK that are 'on a million pounds', but the perception itself should cause concern.

Future engagement

SUMMARY

Despite huge concerns that young people are less engaged with charity and that this may lead to a decline in future giving, nearly all the young people in the survey reported that they intend to give to charity in future – either money, time or more likely both – alongside the range of activities they are already engaged in. They would ideally like charities to present them with easier ways of becoming more involved – and being more engaged on a personal level was felt likely to increase the chances of giving as well. Most young people do not know how to get more involved with charities, and charities may be missing out on the untapped potential of young people willing to get involved in building social capital.

WHAT WILL THEY GIVE?

Some of the young people in the focus groups had no income; many earned very little or had only recently started earning. How do they see themselves best contributing to and getting involved in charity? Do they envisage giving money or time to charity in future? If so, do they see it becoming a regular part of their lives, or is charitable engagement perceived as being an occasional, spur of the moment, occurrence?

The good news is that a massive 96 per cent of the young people surveyed intend to give to charity in future (see Table 4). As one focus group participant commented:

> *If you've been blessed with it, you should give it back to the community that haven't been blessed with it.* (Unemployed, London, 19-24)

In future, young people are most likely to give a bit of both time and money to charity (58 per cent), while 33 per cent intend to give money and 5 per cent intend to give time. Only 4 per cent said that they would give neither time nor money to charity in the future.

Table 4 Future giving intentions of respondents to survey

In the future I will give ... to charity	Proportion agreeing (%)
Both time and money to charity	58
Money only	33
Time only	5
Neither time nor money	4

However, there are some potential constraints upon the foreseen goodwill of young people.

IT DEPENDS HOW EASY IT IS ...

Many young people expressed the opinion that the easier involvement is, the more likely they would be to become engaged in charitable activities, as this conversation shows:

> *I mean we all lead pretty busy lives.*
>
> *I'd probably do that sort of Fairtrade thing because that's easy, you don't have to change your routine too much.*
>
> *I reckon direct debit.*
>
> *I think if there was a programme going on in my village, I'd try and help with that.* (College, South-West, 16–19)

IF SOMETHING HAPPENS TO PROMPT ME ...

Many young people in the focus groups thought that the most likely reason for giving in future is being asked, or being responsive to a prompt in the form of either personal or world events:

> *Something needs to happen; people are very selfish and self-centred.* (Employed, North-West, 19–24)
>
> *If there'd been a crisis, like a flood in Africa, and they were having a special collection to send aid out straight away, then I'd be much more likely to give extra money then.* (University Christian Union, Scotland, 18–22)
>
> *If you are homeless and get help from a charity then you think I will give something back. If you were in that situation, you help someone now who is in that situation.* (Unemployed, London, 19–24)

IF I AM INVOLVED AND GET SOMETHING OUT OF IT ...

Many young people in the focus groups said that they would be more inclined to give by getting actively involved:

> *I'd be more willing to do fundraising events than just give £2 per month; you get something out of it – perhaps I'm selfish ...* (College, South-East, 17–18)
>
> *I think it depends on what your state of mind is to start with. As you get older you've got more responsibilities anyway, like house, car, family, so you might not necessarily give a lot more, but you might just continue.* (Employed, Wales, 19–24)

Some participants stated, however, that they would not know how to get involved with charities:

> *I wouldn't know how to volunteer for a charity, I wouldn't know how to go about it. I can't do something that would require me during the day, but I wouldn't mind doing something a couple of evenings, but I wouldn't know how, what to do sort of thing.* (Employed, Wales, 19–24)

I wouldn't really know how to get involved, unless you go into Oxfam. (College, South-West, 16-19)

The good news is that almost all the young people surveyed (96 per cent) intend to give to charity in future, as Table 4 shows. But does this intention come with any strings? The Giving Campaign found that only 6 per cent of 11–16 year olds felt that they would never give money, and 8 per cent said they would not give time in the future, although most were undecided.

HOW CAN CHARITIES ENGAGE YOUNG PEOPLE IN FUTURE?

Young people in the survey were asked what one thing would be most likely to get them to give money to charity in future. Table 5 shows how they rated the importance of the list of responses.

Table 5 Factors likely to engage young people in charitable giving

What one thing is most likely to get you to give money to charity in future?	Proportion of young people rating this as most important (%)
Knowing that the charity spends the money effectively and makes a difference	25
Nothing, I will give anyway	22
Having lots more money	18
Having a strong link with a charity or cause	16
Having a job	14
If their advertising is good/persuasive	2
Nothing, I won't give anyway	2
If a celebrity I know and admire supports them	<1

The ability to make a difference to society through charitable giving is the single most important factor mentioned here (by one-quarter of respondents), although there is a wide spread of other factors that are almost equally important. It should be very heartening for charities and others to see that almost as many young people (over one-fifth of respondents) will give in future in any case. Having more money is seen as less important in young people's decision to give, and this probably indicates not only that they expect to have enough money in future to be able to give something (the majority expect to be richer than their parents at age 25, according to an Observer/YouGov Poll in 2002), but also that their future giving may hinge on a more tangible engagement with charity. Indeed, it should be noted that having a strong link with a charity is a relatively strong factor in future giving in this survey. All the main factors listed show that young people's attitudes towards giving in future appear to be very similar to those of adults'. If care is taken to address the manner in which they are approached and opportunities offered to them, young people show enthusiasm for being engaged with charity and charities now and in the future.

Summary of findings

Perceptions of 'charity'

- Young people define 'charity' and 'giving' more widely than formal organised charitable activities, focusing more on engagement through active involvement.

- Charity is not seen as something only charities do; 'helping' others in the community informally was also seen as an important charitable act. Neighbourliness or something akin to citizenship was therefore seen as a positive value, while giving time in general was seen as demanding a greater effort than giving money, and was often perceived as a more valuable gift.

Giving to charity

- Giving money to charity is not young people's first impulse in spending money; many feel constrained by a lack of income and the competition of more immediate personal needs.

- Young people are themselves engaged in a wide variety of activities that come under a wider definition of 'charity', better defined as 'altruistic engagement': these activities range from giving goods to charity shops to buying the *Big Issue* and taking part in charity events.

- Young people believe that people-based causes are what they should most give money to (e.g. medical research and care, children's causes and aid for developing countries). They will give as readily to international causes as to local ones, although some have less confidence in long-distance charity, as they can't see the good they do for themselves.

- Compared with an adult population, they rate causes dealing with homelessness, education and young people higher, and heritage and museums and religious causes lower.

- Young people feel very strongly that it is just as much their responsibility to give as older age groups'; the survey revealed that they gave an average of £6.94 in one month, which compares favourably with national adult giving of around £11.82, when relative income is taken into account.

- The most common form of giving money to charity among young people is sponsorship.

Relating to charities

- There is a feeling among young people that the emphasis of charities on raising money can be quite disempowering, as they feel that they have a limited amount to give and that they have more to offer than money.

- Almost half of the young people in the survey thought that there were too few opportunities to give time, while only one-fifth felt that there were too few opportunities to give money to charity.

- Many also felt that the opportunities available were inappropriate to them. For example, just under a third of young people (32 per cent) recycled in the last month, although only 2 per cent rated the environment as their most important charitable cause. This may mean that, although the environment is an important issue for young people, giving to charity is not viewed as the best way of dealing with their environmental concerns.

- Young people are generally positive about charities and their effectiveness in tackling needs by distributing funds, providing care and support, campaigning and raising awareness, and by filling the gaps left by government funding.

- Young people want more information from charities about how to get involved with them. Some believe that charities should put more emphasis on engaging with young people on their terms.

- They find charity advertisements informative and, although many do not have credit cards and are therefore unable to give, the adverts may make them more inclined to give through other methods next time.

- Young people trust charities more than companies or the government and generally believe them to be more effective than either of these in helping to solve society's problems.

- Young people feel that the government has some duty of care in providing welfare services and in using their power to change things judiciously (e.g. in the case of Third World debt, many feel that only the government can have a major impact), although some doubt was expressed about their actual efficacy in doing so.

- Despite their dislike of being approached to give on the streets (a reaction they share with the general population, and which extends to face-to-face fundraisers), young people will often give on the street to registered charities and others (e.g. beggars and *Big Issue* sellers). They also think that the idea of regular giving to charities (such as the direct debits fundraisers promote) is good.

Future engagement

● Young people want more information from charities about what they do with their money and how donations effect change. They also believe that having more information would encourage them to give more in future.

● The future looks relatively bright: the vast majority of young people say that they will give in future – either money or time, more likely both. Young people would be more readily engaged, however, if it were easier to become more involved. Such engagement will be beneficial to both young people and charities.

Conclusions and recommendations

Official surveys of giving show young people to be the least likely age group to give to charity. The research reported here, however, suggests the need to take a broader view when looking at young people's engagement. It seems likely that the real variety of young people's contributions may not be recorded by these official surveys, for a number of reasons, and researchers, charities, voluntary organisations, and society more widely need to look at 'charity' more broadly if the term is to include young people more. This would change the ways in which charities relate to young people and young people relate to them.

Are young people disaffected or disenfranchised? Previous research has shown that there is a general decline in engagement in society among all age groups, and that this is particularly marked in the young. The research reported here is the first explicitly to highlight lack of opportunity as a reason for the apparent lack of engagement of young people. Charities need to realise that, in concentrating their efforts on those people with higher incomes, they may not only be missing out on a huge untapped resource of enthusiastic young people but also burning their bridges when it comes to engaging these youngsters in future. As one focus group participant commented:

> *It's all about intention. If you don't get it when you are young, this feeling that I have to give, and there is a reason why I have to give, it won't come to you when you are older.* (University, South-East, 19-21)

Charities need to engender this feeling with an inclusive approach to young people's engagement: giving money should not always be seen as the most important or appropriate response and, where money *is* required, information about the impact of donations should be given. This might also involve, for example, adapting existing approaches to 'charity' and 'giving' to encompass the wide range of activities that young people engage in on a charitable basis, and include accepting that many young people may favour more radical and active solutions to some problems.

In cultivating such a relationship with young people, charities can make young people feel that they are included, valued and that they have a part to play in society.

This study set out to explore young people's relationship with charity and giving and in particular to investigate the apparent decline in their giving of money. The main findings are outlined in the previous section, and the implications and recommendations arising from these are discussed below.

Perceptions of 'charity' – new approaches

Charity is not a topic at the forefront of young people's minds, and it is not the first thing they'd think to do with their money. When it is discussed, however, they have a well-developed sense of what charity is and what charities do, and have a favourable view of charities' role in raising awareness, and helping people and situations. They think that the charity sector does more good in society than government or business, and have greater trust in charities than in the institutions of the other two sectors.

Defining 'charity' and 'giving' too narrowly excludes much of what young people see as important to them and the society they live in. Young people define the concept of 'charity' and 'giving' more widely than formal organised charitable activity, and this suggests a need for new approaches if these concepts are to be more relevant to what young people are actually doing today.

New approaches need to be taken to the concepts of 'giving' and 'charity', to be more inclusive of the broad range of activities that young people are engaged in (not just giving money). Official surveys of giving need to become more inclusive to recognise and measure the real contributions of young people, in all their variety. Charities that target young people as potential donors only are being too short-sighted and risk alienating a group many of whom already feel marginalised. Charities, and society generally, need to consider 'charity' more broadly to include young people's achievements.

Although there has been considerable effort recently by government and others to boost volunteering opportunities for young people, it appears that many young people still believe there are not enough opportunities to give time: this needs to be addressed.

Giving to charity – counting the contribution

Young people are engaged in a wide range of activities that could be described as 'altruistic', 'socially responsible', 'ethical economics', 'citizenship' or 'charitable', but which may not necessarily be counted under the more formal banner of 'charity' (these activities include recycling, giving old goods to charity shops, giving to beggars, buying fairly traded goods and campaigning about issues).

The current methods surveys use to measure giving underestimate the contributions made by young people. Popular forms of raising and giving money to charity among young people are, for example, sponsorship (the most popular) and giving through company events (e.g. annual sponsored charities, Comic Relief or Children in Need events) and events organised at their colleges (such as 'rag week', charity cloak rooms, and informal collections). Current surveys will fail to measure many of these collections or, if they do, may not attribute them to the young people themselves but to the company or other adults organising them.

A financial value could also be attached to other contributions made by young people that are not currently counted in giving surveys – for example, the giving of goods to charity shops, recycling goods, and buying fair trade products.

Young people perceive that many charities tend to concentrate on the monetary aspects of giving. They know that money is a crucial part of charity and feel that people should give to support charity; however, most young people feel that they haven't got much money, and that charities should try to get them involved in other ways, for example by giving other goods, getting involved in events or helping out ('volunteering').

This points to a need to widen the definition of giving as officially measured in current surveys, which could radically alter the current picture of giving to charity, and young people's position within it. Findings from the Home Office Citizenship Survey show that young people (16–24) participate in clubs and groups more than the rest of the population, although they are least likely to engage with more formal civic and governmental structures. This dichotomy held true for volunteering, as young people were nearly twice as likely to volunteer informally (e.g. helping friends or neighbours) than formally in organisations or charities.

> Young people's engagement in a wide variety of altruistic activities should be celebrated. Activities such as recycling, giving goods to charity shops, and campaigning are forms of citizenship that should be formally recognised.
>
> In addition, young people may not always feel that giving money is the best way to tackle some issues, considering instead that active involvement can be more effective: for example, many more young people actively recycle than give money to environmental charities. Many others feel that only government can tackle some problems effectively and that lobbying is therefore a more efficient way of helping than giving money. Charities need to build on existing interests and try to enlist young people's need for action alongside the charity's need for donations. Charities should also note that involvement with a charity generally leads to higher donation levels from those engaged individuals.

THE GENERATION GAP

Recent research by the Giving Campaign showed that young people aged between 11 and 16 are very engaged in giving and in other charitable activities largely through formal mechanisms and through their schools. Research with adults has shown that giving is also relatively strong around the age of 30 and above, when adults become engaged in the kinds of social and formal networks that encourage giving and involvement.

This study found that 16–24 year olds have a tendency to fall into the gap between these age groups, in terms not only of years but also of opportunities for formal charitable activity. The decreased involvement in formal structures at this age may play a large part in young people's apparent dissociation with society, manifested in this instance in a lack of formal engagement with charities and giving.

In spite of this, the amount of 'altruistic' activities young people actually engage in is considerable!

> To engage young people, charities need to offer the kinds of opportunity that young people will find attractive. This research has revealed the specific gap in opportunities for relevant engagement noticeable in this 16–24 year group, and identified this as a possible reason for the apparent lack of engagement of young people. Charities need to find out more about how young people feel they can make a contribution at the intermediate stage between leaving school and becoming established in the kinds of social network that may encourage giving at an older age. They need to acknowledge the value of young people's support and to channel it in ways that go beyond giving money or beyond a narrowly defined set of volunteering opportunities. Charities need to give young people the right kind of opportunity to become engaged in the issues that they are tackling. Charities need to explore whether young people want to engage in a more active way with the work of charities.

RESPONDING TO FUNDRAISING

Several charity marketing and fundraising methods appear either to slightly annoy young people or to affect them insufficiently to stimulate giving. Advertisements, sponsored activities and big charity events are more popular than face-to-face collections and celebrity or business endorsements. Contrary to some beliefs, many young people seem put off by face-to-face fundraising methods, finding them intrusive and guilt inducing, and they do not discriminate between beggars and charity collectors. The vast majority, however, like the idea of giving a small regular monthly amount by direct debit – even if this is an arrangement they feel able to commit to only in the future. Young people view celebrities' involvement in charity fundraising ambivalently, but do not see it as something that would greatly encourage them to give (though younger respondents were more likely to be influenced by celebrities than those slightly older) – they are wary of some celebrities 'just doing it for the publicity'.

Young people are the most brand-conscious age group and generation and the one that is the target of most marketing. They know the power of advertising and respond intelligently to it. Charity advertising is generally seen as positive awareness raising, although many feel unable to respond directly. Large fundraising events such as Children in Need and Comic Relief are seen as very positive ways for young people to become involved and to see where the money goes.

> Charities need to find out which fundraising techniques young people feel comfortable with and accept that young people are willing to get involved if they believe they are seen as more than 'second class' donors. Charities should not assume that young people have no views on the ways in which they are approached, or on what is appropriate or inappropriate.

Relating to charities

Young people want an active involvement with charities' work and they want to see and understand what charities do with their money. They seem to understand the constraints on what charities can do. However, although they generally trust charities more than either the government or companies, young people have some concerns about charity spending. They want to see evidence of the difference the money given has made (especially when it comes to their own money), and a number cite knowing that the money was spent well and made a difference as the thing most likely to make them give in the future. Overall, however, the vast majority of young people trust charities to spend their money well.

Young people share a cautious optimism about charities, which needs to be built upon and encouraged. Their scepticism is, for the most part, healthy and reasoned, and they are not the only group wanting greater openness and accountability from the charitable sector. Young people are likely to be generally positive about charities and are less critical in many ways than other age groups. Charities should capitalise on this positivity while these people are still young, in order to build a more solid relationship with them when they are older.

> Charities need to provide young people with tangible evidence of what they do with their money. Young people generally believe that charities do good for society, and that giving money, time and other assets to charities are good things to do. They generally trust charities to do the right thing but feel that they would be more inclined to give money if they knew what happened to the donations; this is particularly true of charities whose work is overseas. Young people need reassurance of the impact of donations in places where they cannot see it for themselves. Getting young people more involved with the whole charitable process would provide opportunities to see this at first hand.

Charities need to make clear to young people what their role is in relation to other agencies (such as government) and what value they add, since many young people are clearly confused about charities' potential and actual contribution in some cases. Some young people may feel strongly about certain issues where they think change is needed, but may be unsure how change can best be achieved. Charities would do well to capitalise on young people's desire to change the world – and they are in a good position to do so, as young people trust charities to be more effective than either the public or private sector.

Future engagement

Despite huge concerns that young people are less engaged with charity and that this may lead to a decline in future giving, nearly all the young people in the survey reported that they intend to give to charity in future – either money, time or, more likely, both. They would ideally like charities to present them with easy ways of becoming more involved, and being more engaged on a personal level was felt to increase the chances of giving as well. Most young people do not know how to get more involved with charities.

Charities should recognise what a huge resource pool young people are, and work out how to tap into this goldmine effectively, sensitively, and co-operatively. If young people are not engaged and motivated, the voluntary sector and the wider community will lose out on a huge amount of trust, interest and potential contribution. Charities are the ideal catalysts to engage a generation increasingly antipathetic to traditional involvement in society.

The new citizenship curriculum offers charities further opportunities to engage young people and inform them about their work. Similar opportunities to engage exist in other forms of contact with education, e.g. work experience and sandwich courses. Charities will benefit not only directly from the input of young people in time and effort but also because engagement often leads to greater giving. In addition, by offering more opportunities for young people to get involved on the ground, whether short term or long term (e.g. volunteering during gap years), charities may encourage young people to see the voluntary sector as a viable and interesting career path.

Wider implications

FOR POLICY MAKERS, TEACHERS, YOUTH WORKERS, AND OTHERS DEALING WITH YOUNG PEOPLE

Young people need to be encouraged to engage with charity on terms that allow them to be pro-active, creative and to make a difference. The success of the Millennium Volunteers programme has shown that such schemes can promote engagement with the community and foster social capital, thereby reducing youth detachment and petty crime. Young people have a lot of opinions and ideas about charities and more widely about world situations, but feel they are not often given the opportunity to express these views. The introduction of citizenship into the National Curriculum in September 2002 may help in this respect, but teachers, policy makers and youth workers still have an active role to play in this process.

FOR EMPLOYERS

Young people need to be encouraged to become involved in charity events organised in or by the workplace, giving maximum opportunity for them to be involved at all stages (e.g. consultation on the choice of charity and the nature of the event), which will encourage participation in running the event. Using charity events may also be a way for employers to boost employee morale and staff cohesion, as well as enhancing their own reputation.

FOR FUNDERS

Evidence from the Millennium Volunteers programme, from this (and other similar) research, and from that of the Giving Campaign has shown that young people are receptive and enthusiastic if approached in the right way. This report has demonstrated not only the need for greater investment in young people, but also the great value that can be found by engaging young people in society in innovative ways. Funders of schemes for young people – such as local and national government, trusts and foundations – should look at ways of engaging young people in society in innovative ways. This report has demonstrated not only the need for greater investment in young people, but also the great potential for young people to give something back.

THE HOPE FOR THE FUTURE?

The findings indicate that there is much to be learned from young people on how they view 'charity', and how they see their own role in civil society, and their current and future relationship with charities.

Widening our understanding of charitable giving means recognising and celebrating the fact that young people do a lot more than they are sometimes given credit for in society. We also need to provide opportunities for young people to become engaged with forms of citizenship and building social capital. It is vital for the charity, voluntary and community sector to address young people's concerns, as the future of the sector and the shape of civil society depend on the input of today's young people.

References

Anderson, C. (2001) 'Tips on face-to-face fundraising', *Guardian* Society, 18 July.

Ashdown Group (2001) 'Demographic Profile of Oxfam Supporters: Brand Tracking Research Results' April/May.

Banks, J. and Tanner, S. (1997) *The State of Donation*. London: IFS.

Bowers, S. (2000) 'Children seen and clearly heard as parents consult on lifestyle choice', *Guardian*, 31 July.

BSA (1993, 1995) British Social Attitudes Survey (unpublished reports). West Malling: CAF.

Buckley, D. J. (2002) 'Saddle sore, but it's all for a good cause', *Observer*, Escape, 24 March.

CAF/IFS (2000) 'Briefing Paper 7: Individual Giving'. *Dimensions 2000* online: www.cafonline.org/research/ind_giving.cfm

CAF/IR/NCVO (1999) *Research Briefing: Charity Tax Review*. London: CAF/NCVO.

Charity Commission (2002) *Giving Confidence in Charities*. London: Stationery Office.

Davis Smith, J. (1997) *The 1997 National Survey of Volunteering*. London: National Centre for Volunteering.

Davis Smith, J. (1999) 'Poor marketing or the decline of altruism? Young people and volunteering in the United Kingdom', *International Journal of Nonprofit and Voluntary Sector Marketing*, 4:4: 372–77.

DETR (1998) 'Where does public spending go? Pilot study to analyse the flows of public expenditure into local areas'. London: DETR.

Giddens, A. (1997) *Sociology* 3rd edn. Cambridge: Polity.

Graham, J. and Bowling, B. (1995) 'Young people and crime: Home Office Research Study'. No. 145. London: Stationery Office.

Guardian Unlimited Money (2001) 'Young shrug off debt worries', *Guardian*, 27 April: http://www.guardian.co.uk/Archive/Article/0,4273,4176597,00.html.

Guide Association (2001) *Girls and Citizenship*. London: The Guide Association.

Jas, P. (2002) 'How the general public gives' in Walker *et al.* (eds) *A Lot of Give: Trends in charitable giving for the 21st Century*. London: Hodder & Stoughton.

Jas, P., Wilding, K., Wainwright, S., Passey, A. and Hems, L. (2002) *The UK Voluntary Sector Almanac*. London: NCVO Publications.

King, A. (2002) 'Idle and high on drugs? Not us, say today's youth'. *Daily Telegraph*, 1 July.

Klein, N. (2000) *No Logo*. London: Flamingo.

Kumar, U. (1993) *Poverty and Inequality in the UK and the Effects in Children*. London: NCB.

McCurry, P. (2000) 'Young people targeted by Year of Volunteers campaign', *Guardian*, 9 November.

NOP Consumer Research (1994) Survey for *Super Marketing*: www.fairtrade.org/consumer.

Office of National Statistics (2001a) *Labour Market: New Earnings Survey 2001*. London: ONS.

Office of National Statistics (2001b) *Social Trends*. London: The Stationery Office.

Pharoah, C. & Walker, C. (2002) 'An overview of tax-effective giving' in Walker *et al.* (eds) *A Lot of Give: Trends in charitable giving for the 21st Century*. London: Hodder & Stoughton.

Pharoah, C. (1997) 'The generation game', *Charity*, December 1997: 28–29.

Pharoah, C. (2002a) 'How much do people give to charity, and who are the donors?' in Walker *et al.* (eds) *A Lot of Give: Trends in charitable giving for the 21st Century*. London: Hodder & Stoughton.

Pharoah, C. (2002b) *Dimensions 2002: Update of CAF's top 500 fundraising charities*. West Malling: CAF.

Putnam, (1995) 'Bowling Alone: America's declining social capital', *Journal of Democracy*, January.

Ramrayka, L. (2001) 'Charities urged to woo gap year volunteers', *Guardian*, 16 August.

The Economist (1997) *Pocket Britain in Figures*. London: Profile Books.

Walker, C., Pharoah, C., Jas, P., Passey, A. and Romney-Alexander, D. (eds) (2002) *A Lot of Give: Trends in charitable giving for the 21st Century*. London: Hodder & Stoughton.

Walker, D. (2001) 'Plunge in turnout follows pattern of past decade', *Guardian*, 9 June.

Ward, L. (2002) 'Tories take direct line in hunt for youth vote', *Guardian*, 5 February.

White, M. (1998) 'Irvine urges young to turn away from "don't care" culture', *Guardian*, 28 January.

Willcocks, S. (2002) 'What will £110,000 buy you'? *Guardian*, 5 July.

Wintour, P. (2002) 'Labour inquest on membership loss'. *Guardian*, 29 January.

Appendices

1 Charities mentioned by young people

List of charities spontaneously mentioned by young people in the research, with the number of groups that mentioned them. The list excludes Fairtrade, Comic Relief and Children in Need, because these were referred to in the topic guide.

Oxfam – 7	NSPCC – 5
Cancer Research UK – 7[1]	RSPCA – 4
Big Issue – 5	Barnardo's – 3

The following were all mentioned once in the research:

Acorns	Red Cross
Amnesty International	Ron Smith Cancer Centre
Christian Aid	Roy Castle Lung Cancer Foundation
Fix 2000	Salvation Army
Greenpeace	Samaritans
Help the Aged	Scope
Islamic Relief	Shelter
MacMillan Cancer Relief	Tommy's
Mercy Ships	UNICEF
National Trust	WaterAid
Operation Christmas Child	World Vision
'Poppy Appeal'	Young Muslims UK

Some countries or regions were also named as worthwhile causes:

Afghanistan	Palestine
Africa	Romania
Bangladesh	Somalia
Ethiopia	Sudan
Glasgow	the 'Third World'.
London	

Some medical and social service causes were also mentioned (without referring to specific charities):

Air ambulance	Epilepsy
AIDS	Giving blood
Alcohol abuse	Heart diseases

---

1 In the majority of cases, it was not clear that Cancer Research UK was being referred to; most references were generically to 'cancer research'.

Alzheimer's
Blind people
Brain injuries
Breast cancer
Deaf people
Drug abuse
Elderly people

Homeless people
Leukaemia
Multiple sclerosis
Muslim schools
Respite care
Women's refuges

2 The focus groups

The focus groups were selected to include a wide variety of settings that served as access points to a cross-section of young people in the selected age group. They varied along three dimensions: the type or category of the group; the geographical location of the group (see map); and whether the participants could be described as coming from an urban, semi-urban, semi-rural or rural area. The locations were balanced to reflect geographical spread, differing cultures and communities and differing socio-economic characteristics as shown over the page.

As can be seen, a very balanced gender mixture was achieved, and a relatively representative balance of ethnic origin (given that 'ethnic minority groups have a younger age structure than the white population'.[2]) although the sample perhaps rather over-represents the young Asian population. A good age spread was also achieved.

---

2 ONS, 2001b.

Category	Location	Setting	N	Age range	(n)	Gender (M/F)	Ethnicity (adjudged)	(n)
Employed – Loop customer service centre (Yorkshire Water Services)	Outside Bradford, North-East England	Semi-urban	8	17 18 20 21 22 23	1 1 3 1 1 1	F (3) M (5)	Asian Black White	– – 8
Employed – Iceland Foods	Deeside, Wales	Semi-rural	4	19 21 24	1 1 2	F (2) M (2)	Asian Black White	– – 4
University Christian Union	St Andrews, Scotland	Semi-urban	9	19 20 21 22 23	1 2 3 2 1	F (7) M (2)	Asian Black White	1 – 8
Unemployed – New Deal participants	London, South-East England	Urban	8	18 19 20 21 23 24	1 2 1 1 1 2	F (3) M (5)	Asian Black White	4 2 2
College, agricultural course students	Bicton, Devon, South-West England	Rural	9	16 18 19 20	5 1 2 1	M (6) F (3)	Asian Black White	– – 9
College (6th form)	Worthing, South-East England	Semi-urban	6	17 18	5 1	F (3) M (3)	Asian Black White	– – 6
Employed – Royal & Sun Alliance	Liverpool, North West England	Urban	8	19 21 22 23 24	1 1 1 2 3	F (5) M (3)	Asian Black White	– – 8
University Islamic Society	Royal Holloway University, Surrey, South-East England	Semi-urban	5	18 20 21	1 2 2	F (2) M (3)	Asian Black White	5 – –
College – Special Needs 6th form	Selly Oak, Birmingham, Midlands	Urban	13	16 17 18 19	6 5 1 1	F (5) M (8)	Asian Black White	– 1 12
TOTALS		**Rural (1)** **Semi-rural (1)** **Semi-urban (4)** **Urban (3)**	70	**16** **17** **18** **19** **20** **21** **22** **23** **24**	**11** **11** **6** **8** **9** **8** **5** **5** **7**	**F (33)** **M (37)**	**Asian** **Black** **White**	**10** **3** **57**

3 Focus group topic guide

INTRODUCTORY STAGE

Ice-breaker

- Name? Age? (going around the group)

- If you found £10 you didn't think you had, would you give anything to charity?

KEY QUESTIONS

Defining charity

- What is charity? (Write down a few words or phrases to describe what it means to you, then discuss with the group.)

- What does the word 'charity' mean to you?

- What is the role/purpose of charity (in today's society)?

Vignette – everyone comment on

- Who is the most 'charitable' of these people?

- What sort of person is A, B, C, D?

- What other ways of giving are there? Is that 'charity'?

Causes

- What causes are important to give to?

- What kinds of situation can be helped by 'charity'?

- Which issues do you think can be helped by the money people give to charity?

- (Try to move the discussion beyond the vignettes and steer it onto charitable issues and money.)

- Does charity begin at home?

- When you think of giving to charity, do you prefer to help situations or people which are local, British or international?

Giving

- Whose responsibility is it to give (to charity)?

- Who should give money to help these things we've been discussing?

- [prompt] Should everyone give money? Should no one give?

- [prompt] Is it just adults who should give? Or wealthy people? Or should the government help out more?

- [prompt] What does it depend on?

Charity marketing

- How does the way charities raise money affect the likelihood of your giving?

- [prompt] fundraising methods – face to face

- [prompt] Advertising

- [prompt] Role models/celebrities/private companies sponsoring

- [prompt] Sponsorship – i.e. sponsored run, swim, cycle, etc.

- [prompt] Events – e.g. Comic Relief/Children in Need

- What kind of relationship do you want with charities?

- Would you like to be more involved with charities?

Future intentions

- When you have more money, do you think you will give more to charity?

- [prompt] Should you?

FINAL QUESTION?

- Where would you like to see this research published?/Where would be a good place to see it published? (dissemination)

4 Quantitative survey questionnaire

The survey participants were selected to be nationally representative of the 16–24 year age group in Great Britain. Five hundred and ninety (590) young people were surveyed in face-to-face CAPI interviews (Computer Assisted Personal Interviewing) using a number of questions placed in the ACCESS national omnibus. The sample was weighted according to gender, age, employment status of housewives (and whether they had children), social class and standard region. The questions asked are laid out below.

1 In the last month have you done any of the following?

- Recycled used materials (e.g. glass, cans, paper, clothes)
- Given any money to charity as part of a regular giving arrangement (every week or month e.g. by direct debit or church collection, etc.)
- Given money to beggars in the street
- Bought the *Big Issue*
- Given any money to [a registered] charity spontaneously in the street (e.g. to people with charity tins or buckets)
- Given any money in direct response to a charity advertisement or appeal in the media
- Given any goods to be sold in a charity shop or charity jumble sale
- Bought anything in a charity shop
- Bought any Fairtrade goods
- Sponsored someone else to do something for charity
- Spent time doing something for a charity (e.g. a sponsored swim, walk, etc., volunteered in a charity shop)
- Campaigned about an issue which you feel strongly about (e.g. written letters or taken part in a demonstration)
- Don't know
- None of these

2 Could you estimate how much you gave to charity in total in the last month?

- Nothing
- Less than 50p
- 50p–99p
- £1–£1.99
- £2–£2.99

- £3–£4.99
- £5–£9.99
- £10–£19.99
- £20–£29.99
- £30–£39.99
- £40–£49.99
- More than £50
- Don't know

3 How much do you agree or disagree with the following statements?

Strongly agree

Slightly agree

Neither agree nor disagree

Slightly disagree

Strongly disagree

Don't know

- *I don't have enough money to give to charity.*
- *I don't believe giving to charity is the answer to society's problems.*
- *I prefer to give time to charity than to give money.*
- *Rich people have more responsibility to give to charity than me.*
- *I trust most charities to use my money well if I give a donation.*
- *If I haven't heard of the charity before, I won't give to them.*
- *Charity advertisements or appeals make me more likely to give to that charity.*
- *People of my age have just as much responsibility to give to charity as older people.*
- *I use the Internet a lot to look up information about charities.*
- *I don't like being approached in the streets to give money.*
- *If my college or employer organised a charity event, I would get involved.*
- *If a celebrity who I admire gets involved with a charity, I would be more likely to give to that charity.*
- *I think giving a small amount every month is a good way to give to charity.*
- *There aren't enough opportunities for me to give money to charity.*
- *There aren't enough opportunities for me to give my time to charity.*

4 In the future what do you think you will give to charity?

- Money
- Time

- A bit of both

- Neither

- Don't know

5 What one thing is most likely to get you to give money to charity in future?

- Nothing, I will give anyway.

- Having lots more money.

- Having a job.

- Having a strong link with a charity or cause.

- Knowing that the charity spends the money effectively and makes a difference.

- If their advertising is good/persuasive.

- If a celebrity I know and admire supports them.

- Nothing, I won't give anyway.

- Don't know.

- Other: specify.

6 Which ONE of the following charitable causes do you think is most important to give money to?

- Medical research and/or medical care

- Children and/or young people

- Disabled people

- Elderly people

- The Third World/Overseas aid

- Animals

- The environment (e.g. green issues)

- Religious organisations

- Education

- Heritage (e.g. stately homes)

- Homeless people in this country

- Museums, music, art, etc.

- Don't know

- None of these

About CAF

CAF, Charities Aid Foundation, is a registered charity with a unique mission – to increase the substance of charity in the UK and overseas. To do this, CAF provides financial services designed to meet the specific needs of voluntary organisations and those who support them.

As an integral part of its activities, CAF works to raise standards of management in voluntary organisations. This includes leading the debate on accountability, providing consultancy and grants to improve the infrastructure of small to medium-sized charities, organising seminars and workshops, and hosting its own Annual Conference and Exhibition, the largest regular gathering of key people from within the voluntary sector.

In addition, since 1995, CAF has been a leading figure in the development of online resources for charities. Its two most recent websites, AllAboutGiving.org and GiveNow.org, enable any recognised UK charity, regardless of whether it has a web presence, to target entirely new audiences and fundraise online for free.

For decades, CAF has led the way in developing tax-effective services to donors, and these are now used by more than 350,000 individuals and over 3,000 of the UK's leading companies, who between them give £260 million each year to charity.

CAF's unique range of investment and administration services for charities includes the CafCash cheque account and the CAF Gold deposit account, three specialist investment funds for longer-term investment and a full appeals, membership and tax recovery service. Many charities are also using CAF's new Efundraising service, which offers tailored online solutions enabling them to accept tax-effective donations directly from their own websites.

CAF's activities are not limited to the UK, however. Increasingly, CAF is looking to apply the same principles and develop similar services internationally, and has offices and sister organisations in the United States, Bulgaria, Southern and West Africa, Russia, India, Australia and Brussels.

CAF Research is a leading source of information and research on the voluntary sector's income and resources. Its annual publication *Dimensions of the Voluntary Sector*, provides year-on-year updates, and its Research Report series covers a wide range of topics, including benchmarking costs, partnership resources, and trust and company funding. More details on research and publications may be found on *www.CAFonline.org/research*.

For more information about CAF, please visit *www.CAFonline.org*.